City Eggs: *Deviled Eggs for FOODIES/ 60 Deviled Egg Recipes from US Cities*

by Marlene Miles

Freshwater Press

Freshwaterpress9@gmail.com

ISBN: 978-1-967860-27-2

Paperback Version

Copyright 2025, Marlene Miles

All rights reserved. No part of this book may be reproduced, distributed, or transmitted by any means or in any means including photocopying, recording or other electronic or mechanical methods without prior written permission of the publisher except in the case of brief publications or critical reviews.

Table of Contents

Introduction 6

How to Hard Boil Eggs 7

Build the Egg 8

Anchorage Smoked Salmon & Dill Deviled Eggs 11

Asheville Pimento Cheese & Smoked Trout Deviled Eggs 14

Atlanta Hot Lemon Pepper Wing Deviled Eggs 17

Baltimore Crab Cake Deviled Eggs 20

Austin Brisket & Jalapeño Deviled Eggs 23

Bethesda Truffle & Crab Deviled Eggs 26

Birmingham Hot Soul Deviled Eggs 29

Boca Raton Citrus & Avocado Deviled Eggs 32

Boise Rosemary Truffle Deviled Eggs with Crispy Potato Nest 35

Boston Clam Chowder Deviled Eggs 38

Buffalo Hot Wings Deviled Eggs with Bleu Cheese 41

Buffalo Deviled Eggs – Ranch Version 44

Burlington Maple & Cheddar Deviled Eggs 47

Charlotte Pimento Cheese & Pulled Pork Deviled Eggs 50

Charlottesville Goat Cheese & Fig Deviled Eggs 53

Charleston, SC Shrimp & Grits Deviled Eggs 56

Charleston, WV Pepperoni & Sauerkraut Deviled Eggs 59

Cheyenne Bison & Sweet Onion Deviled Eggs 62

Chicago Giardiniera & Salami Deviled Eggs 65

Cincinnati 5-Way Chili Deviled Eggs 68

D.C. Embassy Row Deviled Eggs with Sumac & Tahini 71

Detroit Coney Island Chili & Cheese Deviled Eggs 74

Denver Green Chili & Cheddar Deviled Eggs 77

Des Moines Sweet Corn & Smoked Gouda Deviled Eggs 80

Fargo Wild Mushroom & Caraway Deviled Eggs 83

Galveston Tuna Salad Deviled Eggs 86

Hilton Head Crab & Cajun Deviled Eggs 89

Honolulu Spam Musubi Deviled Eggs 92

Indianapolis Cornbread & Jalapeño Deviled Eggs 95

Jackson BBQ & Pickled Jalapeño Deviled Eggs 98

Kansas City BBQ Deviled Eggs 101

Key West Lime & Cilantro Deviled Eggs 104

Las Vegas Bacon-Wrapped Dates & Manchego Deviled Eggs 107

Lawrence Roasted Beet & Herbed Goat Cheese Deviled Eggs 110

Little Rock Fried Pickle Deviled Eggs 113

Los Angeles Avocado & Sriracha Deviled Eggs 116

Louisville Bourbon Bacon Deviled Eggs 119

Milwaukee Butter Burger Deviled Eggs 122

Minneapolis Wild Rice & Maple-Glazed Bacon Deviled Eggs 125

Morgantown Pepper Jack & Smoked Sausage Deviled Eggs 128

Nashville Hot Chicken Deviled Eggs 131

New Haven White Clam & Herb Deviled Eggs 134

New Orleans Cajun Shrimp Remoulade Deviled Eggs 137

Newport Jazz & Clam Bake Deviled Eggs 140

Newark Jibarito-Inspired Deviled Eggs 143

Niagara Falls Apple & Cheddar Deviled Eggs 146

Omaha Steakhouse Deviled Eggs 149

Philly Cheesesteak Deviled Eggs 152

Portland Lobster & Brown Butter Deviled Eggs 155

Portsmouth Clam & Chive Deviled Eggs 158

Rehoboth Beach Crab & Old Bay Deviled Eggs 161

Richmond Ham & Pimento Deviled Eggs 164

Salt Lake City Honey & Sage Deviled Eggs 167

San Francisco Sourdough & Dungeness Crab Deviled Eggs 170

Santa Fe Tomatillo & Cilantro Deviled Eggs 173

St. Louis Toasted Ravioli & Provel Deviled Eggs 176

Sioux Falls Bison Chili Deviled Eggs 179

Tucson Roasted Poblano & Queso Fresco Deviled Eggs 182

Tulsa Chicken-Fried Steak & White Gravy Deviled Eggs 185

Virginia Beach Old Bay & Fried Clam Deviled Eggs 188

Coffee & Vanilla-Infused Egg Whites + Maple Bacon Filling 191

Maple Espresso Martini 194

Mocktail Maple Espresso Martini 197

Introduction

Welcome to *City Eggs: So Many Cities, So Many Deviled Eggs*—a culinary journey across America's vibrant urban landscapes From the smoky barbecue flavors of Austin to the fresh seafood notes of Portland, each recipe captures the unique spirit and flavor of a beloved city. Whether you're a devoted foodie, an adventurous cook, or someone who just loves a good deviled egg, this collection offers something deliciously unexpected.

These deviled eggs celebrate local traditions, iconic dishes, and the diverse tastes that make each city unforgettable. They're perfect for game days, elegant gatherings, casual parties, or anytime you want to impress with a dish that's both classic and creative.

So grab a platter, gather your favorite people, and let's explore America's cities through these delicious, handcrafted deviled eggs. Here's to the flavors that bring us together—one egg, one city, one story at a time.

Enjoy!

How to Hard Boil Eggs

<u>Eggs for deviled eggs are hardboiled</u>. Yes, absolutely — the eggs used for deviled eggs are **hard-boiled**. Here's the basic process:

1. Place eggs in a saucepan or larger pan starting with cool water. Be sure the water covers the eggs for even cooking.
2. **Hard-boil the eggs** – Bring to a boil, covered or uncovered. Boil them until both the whites and yolks are fully cooked (usually about 10–12 minutes).
3. **Let the cooked eggs rest another 10 to 12 minutes**.
4. **Cool them** – Chill in an ice bath or cold water so they're easier to peel.
5. **Peel and slice** – Cut them in half lengthwise, (usually).
6. **Scoop out yolks** – The yolks are mashed and mixed with other ingredients (like mayo, mustard, etcetera.).
7. **Fill the whites** – Spoon or pipe the creamy yolk mixture back into the whites. You may have noticed without stuffing the eggs that there may not be enough of the yolk mixture to fill the egg whites, but that will never be a problem with these recipes.

Hard-boiled eggs are essential because you need a firm, cooked yolk for that classic deviled texture.

If you have another technique for hard boiling eggs that works for you, use that method. The above information is for cooks who have less experience and may not know how long to cook their eggs for deviled eggs.

Build the Egg

You can be creative with these recipes in ways such as how you fold in the ingredients. Sometimes I like to put a little sauce at the bottom of the egg white so there is a lasting flavor at the bottom of the egg, and at the end of the bite. In this way, all the flavor is not on top. Alternately, you could put the "toppings" on the bottom of the egg half. It won't be as visually appealing, but it will make a great surprise when your guest bites into the egg.

Only a little extra meat, fish, shrimp, or other stuffing will go a long way. So, when you look in the fridge or the pantry and think you have nothing, if you have eggs, you have a lot. You can turn any of these recipes into a full meal because many of them are quite hearty. *Be sure to make your yolk mixture smooth and well-mixed before adding any ingredients like meats and cheeses.

While the images in this book are beautiful, you will reach your own balance of how much meat or other topping you will add for balance and personal preference for appearance and purpose of the egg. If it is an appetizer, you may go very light on the topping. If it is a heartier snack, you will add the amount of topping that fits your gathering or meal.

No matter how you assemble it, each recipe will be very tasty and add a new dimension to your deviled eggs. No matter how you put them together, every guest will be delighted.

Most of these recipes in this book will allow you to create masterpieces. Get your ingredients, take your time, enjoy yourself and wow your family and friends. You'll get more dinner invitations than ever if you show up with one of these amazing deviled egg dishes.

*Hint:

I almost never need to add salt to the yolk mixture of the deviled egg; it's always salty enough on its own except when adding bland ingredients such as avocado. Careful not to oversalt your masterpiece eggs. I would add salt last if needed, especially when adding meets, capers and other potentially salty items to your recipe.

Anchorage Smoked Salmon & Dill Deviled Eggs

Anchorage Smoked Salmon & Dill Deviled Eggs

Cool, clean, and Alaskan chic.

Why It's Uniquely Anchorage:

Anchorage is Alaska's gateway to wilderness and home to fresh seafood, smoked fish, and a rising urban food scene that blends rustic ingredients with upscale presentation. This deviled egg is inspired by **lox and bagels**, but with a wild Alaskan twist—**smoked salmon, fresh dill, and a** touch of lemon. A deviled egg filled with creamy, pale-yellow yolk flecked with dill and topped with a curl of smoked salmon and a sprig of fresh dill.

Elegant, earthy, and bracingly fresh.

Ingredients:

- 12 large eggs
- 1/3 cup mayonnaise
- 1 tsp Dijon mustard
- 1 tsp lemon juice
- 1–2 oz **finely chopped smoked salmon** (cold-smoked preferred)
- 1 tbsp chopped fresh dill
- Salt and black pepper to taste

Optional:

- 1 tsp cream cheese for added richness

- A pinch of lemon zest

Garnish:

- Small piece of smoked salmon
- Sprig of fresh dill
- Optional: microgreens or caper

Instructions:

1. **Boil and Cool the Eggs:**
    - Standard boil, ice bath, peel.
2. **Make the Filling:**
    - Halve eggs, remove yolks.
    - Mash yolks with mayo, mustard, lemon juice, and optional cream cheese.
    - Fold in chopped smoked salmon and dill. Season to taste.
3. **Assemble the Eggs:**
    - Pipe or spoon filling into whites.
4. **Top with Alaskan Elegance:**
    - Garnish with a salmon curl, dill sprig, or microgreens for freshness.

Serving Vibe:

Perfect for a cold plate at brunch, a winter-themed charcuterie board, or a sleek seafood spread with oyster shells and glacier-blue tones.

Asheville Pimento Cheese & Smoked Trout deviled Eggs

Asheville Pimento Cheese & Smoked Trout Deviled Eggs

Creamy, smoky, and perfectly Southern deviled eggs filled with creamy yellow yolk mixed with shredded pimento cheese and finely flaked smoked trout. Each egg is garnished with a small flake of smoked trout, a slice of roasted red pepper (pimento), and fresh chives or parsley.

Why It's Uniquely Asheville:

Asheville is known for its farm-fresh ingredients and artisanal touches. This deviled egg combines the classic Southern **pimento cheese** spread with a smoky twist of local smoked trout, delivering rich, tangy, and smoky flavors that capture Asheville's culinary soul.

Ingredients:

- 12 large eggs
- 1/3 cup mayonnaise
- 1/4 cup shredded pimento cheese
- 2 tbsp finely flaked smoked trout
- 1 tsp lemon juice
- Salt and pepper to taste

Garnish:

- Smoked trout flake

- Pimento slice or tiny roasted red pepper
- Fresh chives or parsley

Instructions:

1. **Boil and Cool the Eggs:**
   Standard: boil, rest, ice bath, peel.

2. **Make the Filling:**
   Mash yolks with mayo, pimento cheese, smoked trout, and lemon juice. Season with salt and pepper.

3. **Assemble the Eggs:**
   Pipe or spoon into egg whites.

4. **Garnish with Mountain Freshness**
   Top with trout flakes, pimento, and fresh herbs.

Serving Vibe:

Serve on a wooden board with craft beers or local cider, surrounded by mountain herbs and artisanal bread for a perfect Appalachian gathering.

Atlanta Hot Lemon Pepper Wing Deviled Eggs

Atlanta Hot Lemon Pepper Wing Deviled Eggs

Spicy, citrusy, and straight-up iconic.

Why It's Uniquely Atlanta:

Atlanta is the undisputed home of the lemon pepper wing—especially the hot variety. From strip club kitchens to upscale brunch menus, hot lemon pepper is the city's most craveable flavor. A deviled egg filled with smooth, yellow yolk mixture flecked with lemon zest and cayenne, topped with a crispy strip of chicken skin or a light dusting of lemon pepper seasoning.

This deviled egg captures that legendary profile with a buttery citrus kick, a touch of heat, and a crispy chicken skin topper if you're feeling extra.

Ingredients:

- 12 large eggs
- 1/3 cup mayonnaise
- 1 tsp yellow mustard
- 1 tsp fresh lemon juice
- 1/2 tsp lemon zest
- 1/4 tsp cayenne or hot sauce (adjust to taste)
- Salt and black pepper to taste
- Optional: dash of garlic powder or paprika

Topping (Choose 1):

- A tiny strip of **crispy chicken skin** (baked or fried)
- A sprinkle of lemon pepper seasoning
- A small lemon zest curl

Instructions:

1. **Boil and Cool the Eggs:**
   Standard method: boil, rest, ice bath, peel.

2. **Make the Filling:**
   Halve eggs and mash yolks with mayo, mustard, lemon juice, zest, cayenne or hot sauce, and seasoning.

3. **Assemble the Eggs:**
   Pipe or spoon into whites.

4. **Garnish Like You Mean It:**
   Top each with crispy chicken skin or a dash of lemon pepper seasoning.

Serving Vibe:

Perfect for a rooftop brunch, music video shoot, or Sunday after church with mimosas and gospel in the background.

Baltimore Crab Cake Deviled Eggs

Baltimore Crab Cake Deviled Eggs

Creamy, briny, and bold—like a crab cake in deviled egg form.

Deviled eggs with a creamy golden filling mixed with crabmeat and Old Bay seasoning, piped into egg whites. Each topped with a flake of crab, a sprinkle of Old Bay, and a chive or lemon zest curl

---

Why It's Uniquely Baltimore:

Baltimore lives and breathes **blue crab**, and this egg brings that energy straight to the plate. With lump crabmeat, Old Bay seasoning, and a bit of Dijon, it's a deviled egg that channels the city's signature dish: the crab cake. No filler—just flavor.

Ingredients:

- 12 large eggs
- 1/3 cup mayonnaise
- 1 tsp Dijon mustard
- 1 tsp lemon juice
- 1/2 tsp Old Bay seasoning (plus more for garnish)
- 3 oz lump crabmeat (picked over for shells)
- Salt and pepper to taste

- Optional: 1 tsp minced scallion or celery for crunch

Garnish:

- Sprinkle of Old Bay
- Small flake of crabmeat or chive tip
- Lemon zest (optional)

Instructions:

1. **Boil and Cool the Eggs:**
   Use the classic method: boil, rest, ice bath, peel.

2. **Make the Filling:**
   Mash yolks with mayo, mustard, lemon juice, and Old Bay. Gently fold in crabmeat and optional veggies. Season with salt and pepper.

3. **Assemble the Eggs:**
   Pipe or spoon into whites.

4. **Garnish Like a Crab Shack Pro:**
   Top with a pinch of crabmeat, extra Old Bay, or a bright garnish like lemon zest or fresh chive.

Serving Vibe:

Serve on a rustic wood board or nautical-themed platter. Ideal for seafood spreads, waterfront gatherings, or game-day bites with a Maryland twist.

Austin Brisket & Jalapeno Deviled Eggs

Austin Brisket & Jalapeño Deviled Eggs

Smoky, spicy, and bursting with Texas flair. Deviled eggs filled with creamy yolk mixture blended with finely chopped smoked brisket and diced jalapeño. Each egg is topped with a small piece of brisket and a thin jalapeño slice.

Why It's Uniquely Austin:

Austin's barbecue scene is legendary, especially its tender, smoky brisket. This deviled egg blends creamy yolks with smoky chopped brisket and a kick of jalapeño heat. It's a perfect bite for the city that knows how to mix flavor and fun.

Ingredients:

- 12 large eggs
- 1/3 cup mayonnaise
- 1 tbsp Dijon mustard
- 2 tbsp finely chopped smoked brisket
- 1 tsp finely diced jalapeño (adjust for heat)
- Salt and pepper to taste

Topping:

- Small piece of chopped brisket

- Thin jalapeño slice
- Optional: sprinkle of smoked paprika or chopped cilantro

Instructions:

1. **Boil and Cool the Eggs:**
   Standard: boil, ice bath, peel.

2. **Make the Filling:**
   Mash yolks with mayo, mustard, chopped brisket, and jalapeño. Season to taste.

3. **Assemble the Eggs:**
   Pipe or spoon filling into whites.

4. **Garnish with Austin Attitude:**
   Top with brisket pieces, jalapeño slices, and fresh herbs.

Serving Vibe:

Serve on a casual wooden board with craft beers and live music vibes. Perfect for food truck festivals or backyard BBQ jams.

Bethesda Truffle & Crab Deviled Eggs

Bethesda Truffle & Crab Deviled Eggs

Luxurious, delicate, and decadently refined.

Deviled eggs filled with creamy yolk mixture blended with Maryland lump crab meat and a subtle drizzle of truffle oil. Each garnished with crème fraîche, fresh chive or microgreens, and a small shaving of black truffle or truffle zest.

Why It's Uniquely Bethesda/Chevy Chase:

This deviled egg blends creamy yolks with rich Maryland crab meat and a subtle touch of truffle oil, delivering a sophisticated flavor perfect for upscale gatherings and elegant soirées.

Ingredients:

- 12 large eggs
- 1/3 cup mayonnaise
- 2 tbsp lump Maryland crab meat, picked over for shells
- 1 tsp truffle oil (use sparingly)
- 1 tsp Dijon mustard
- Salt and white pepper to taste

Garnish:

- Tiny dollop of crème fraîche
- Fresh chive tips or microgreens
- Optional: a small shaving of black truffle or truffle zest

Instructions:

1. **Boil and Cool the Eggs:**
   Standard boil, rest, ice bath, peel.

2. **Make the Filling:**
   Mash yolks with mayo, mustard, and truffle oil. Gently fold in crab meat. Season with salt and white pepper.

3. **Assemble the Eggs:**
   Pipe or spoon filling into whites.

4. **Garnish with Upscale Flair:**
   Add a small dollop of crème fraîche, fresh chives or microgreens, and optional truffle shaving.

Serving Vibe:

Serve on elegant porcelain plates with crystal glassware and soft ambient lighting. Perfect for cocktail parties or art gallery openings.

Birmingham Hot Soul Deviled Eggs

Birmingham Hot Soul Deviled Eggs

Spicy, soulful, and brunch-table ready. A stylish deviled egg set on a matte black platter, filled with creamy golden yolk tinged with hot sauce. Each topped with a crispy collard green chip or a sprinkle of golden cornbread crumble.

Why It's Uniquely Birmingham:

Birmingham is known for its rich civil rights history, its Black-owned soul food spots, and a new wave of elevated Southern cuisine. This deviled egg channels all of that with creamy filling, hot sauce heat, and a crispy collard green or cornbread topping. Its Southern soul meets downtown flair.

Ingredients:

- 12 large eggs
- 1/3 cup mayonnaise
- 1 tsp yellow mustard
- 1 tsp apple cider vinegar
- 1 tsp hot sauce (like Crystal or Tabasco)
- Salt and black pepper to taste
- Optional: pinch of garlic powder or cayenne

Topping Options (choose one or both):

- Crispy collard green shards (baked or fried)

- Crumbled cornbread croutons

Optional Garnish:
- Tiny drop of hot sauce
- Minced chives or parsley

Instructions:

1. **Boil and Cool the Eggs:**
   - Standard method: boil 10–12 minutes, ice bath, peel.

2. **Make the Filling:**
   - Slice eggs and remove yolks.
   - Mash yolks with mayo, mustard, vinegar, and hot sauce.
   - Season with salt, pepper, and optional cayenne or garlic powder.

3. **Assemble the Eggs:**
   - Spoon or pipe into whites.

4. **Top with Soul:**
   - Garnish with a crispy collard green piece or a pinch of cornbread crumble.
   - Add a drop of hot sauce for visual pop.

Serving Vibe:

Serve these on a sleek slate tray with vintage-style toothpicks or gold cocktail forks. Soul food goes uptown.

Boca Raton Citrus & avocado Deviled Eggs

Boca Raton Citrus & Avocado Deviled Eggs

Bright, creamy, and elegantly fresh.

Deviled eggs filled with creamy yolk mixture blended with ripe avocado and fresh citrus juice. Each garnished with chili flakes, a thin strip of citrus zest (lime or orange), and fresh cilantro or microgreens.

Why It's Uniquely Boca Raton:

Boca Raton cuisine celebrates fresh citrus and creamy avocados, reflecting the sunny South Florida lifestyle. This deviled egg blends creamy yolks with ripe avocado and a splash of fresh citrus juice for a bright, smooth bite, topped with a sprinkle of chili flakes for subtle heat.

Ingredients:

- 12 large eggs
- 1/3 cup mayonnaise
- 1/4 cup ripe avocado, mashed
- 1 tbsp fresh lime or orange juice
- Salt and pepper to taste

Topping:

- Sprinkle of chili flakes or smoked paprika

- Thin citrus zest strip (lime or orange)
- Fresh cilantro or microgreens

Instructions:

1. **Boil and Cool the Eggs:**
   Standard boil, ice bath, peel.

2. **Make the Filling:**
   Mash yolks with mayo, mashed avocado, and citrus juice. Season to taste.

3. **Assemble the Eggs:**
   Pipe or spoon filling into whites.

4. **Garnish with Sunny Flair:**
   Top with chili flakes, citrus zest, and fresh herbs.

Serving Vibe:

Serve on a sleek white platter with tropical décor and chilled white wine or mojitos. Perfect for poolside parties or elegant coastal brunches.

Boise Rosemary Truffle Deviled Eggs with Crispy Potato Nest

Boise Rosemary Truffle Deviled Eggs with Crispy Potato Nest

Earthy. Chic. And totally farm-to-table fabulous. A deviled egg filled with creamy rosemary-infused yolk, topped with a delicate nest of golden crispy matchstick potatoes. Optional garnishes include a microgreen or tiny rosemary tip

---

Why It's Uniquely Boise:

Boise's food scene embraces *elevated rustic*—think truffle fries, rosemary focaccia, and hip micro-bakeries. This deviled egg blends that mountain-city sophistication: a creamy filling with rosemary and a hint of truffle oil, crowned with a crisp spiral of matchstick potatoes. It's stylish, fragrant, and ultra-satisfying.

Ingredients:

- 12 large eggs
- 1/4 cup mayonnaise
- 1/2 tsp Dijon mustard
- 1/4 tsp truffle oil (just a drop goes a long way!)
- 1/4 tsp finely minced fresh rosemary
- Salt and black pepper to taste

Topping:

- A nest of **crispy fried matchstick potatoes** (like mini shoestring fries)
- Optional: microgreens or rosemary sprig tip

Instructions:

1. **Boil and Cool the Eggs:**
   Standard method: boil, rest, ice bath, peel.

2. **Make the Filling:**
   Mash yolks with mayo, mustard, truffle oil, and rosemary. Season to taste. It should be creamy, fragrant, and just earthy enough.

3. **Assemble the Eggs:**
   Pipe or spoon filling into whites.

4. **Garnish with a Crispy Nest:**
   Top each egg with a pinch of freshly fried matchstick potatoes. (Use a spiralizer or mandoline and fry in hot oil until golden.) Optional microgreen for flair.

Serving Vibe:

Perfect for a rooftop garden party or a downtown Boise gallery opening. Pairs beautifully with dry cider or sparkling white wine.

Boston Clam Chowder Deviled Eggs

Boston Clam Chowder Deviled Eggs

Creamy, savory, and surprisingly elegant—chowder-inspired and wicked good.

Boston Clam Chowder Deviled Eggs: Each is garnished with crips bacon, thyme, or crushed oyster crackers.

Why It's Uniquely Boston:

Boston is chowder country. From Quincy Market to Beacon Hill, locals love that rich, creamy clam flavor. This deviled egg blends chopped clams, smoky bacon, and a dash of thyme into a silky filling—like a bowl of chowder in one perfect bite. Bonus points for a crispy potato or oyster cracker crunch on top.

Ingredients:

- 12 large eggs
- 1/4 cup mayonnaise
- 1 tsp Dijon mustard
- 1 tsp lemon juice
- 1/2 tsp fresh thyme (or 1/4 tsp dried)
- 1/4 cup finely chopped **cooked clams** (canned or fresh)
- 2 slices cooked **bacon**, finely crumbled

- Salt and black pepper to taste

Optional Garnish:

- Micro-thyme sprig
- Bacon crumble
- Crushed oyster cracker or tiny cube of roasted potato

Instructions:

1. **Boil and Cool the Eggs:**
   Standard method: boil, rest, ice bath, peel.

2. **Make the Filling:**
   Mash yolks with mayo, mustard, lemon juice, and thyme. Stir in chopped clams and bacon. Season to taste.

3. **Assemble the Eggs:**
   Pipe or spoon into egg whites.

4. **Garnish with New England Charm:**
   Add a crisp topping: bacon crumbles, thyme, or crushed oyster crackers.

Serving Vibe:

Serve on a white ceramic tray or driftwood board, with navy-striped napkins and a sea breeze vibe. Great for classy game-day spreads or Cape Cod-inspired brunches.

.Buffalo Hot Wings Deviled Eggs with Bleu Cheese

Buffalo Hot Wings Deviled Eggs with Bleu Cheese

Spicy, tangy, creamy—and topped with **crumbled blue cheese** and a **sliver of celery**—these eggs pack all the flavor of Buffalo wings without the mess. Great for game day or anytime you want to bring the heat. Buffalo Chicken Wings Deviled Eggs, Blue Cheese version.

Optional: Add Buffalo Sauce make spicier

Ingredients:

- 12 large eggs
- 1/3 cup mayonnaise
- 1 tbsp hot sauce (like Frank's Red Hot)
- 1 tsp white vinegar or lemon juice
- 1 tsp Dijon or yellow mustard
- Salt and black pepper to taste
- 2 tbsp finely shredded cooked chicken breast (rotisserie or poached)
- Optional: pinch of garlic powder or cayenne

Garnish:

- Crumbled blue cheese or blue cheese dressing
- Thin celery slivers or chopped scallions
- Dash of paprika or hot sauce drizzle

Instructions:

1. **Boil and peel the eggs:**

   Standard 10–12 minute boil, ice bath, then peel.

2. **Prepare the filling:**
   Slice eggs in half and remove yolks. Mash yolks with mayo, hot sauce, mustard, and vinegar. Add salt, pepper, and optional garlic or cayenne to taste. Fold in shredded chicken.

3. **Assemble the eggs:**
   Spoon or pipe the spicy filling into egg whites.

4. **Add toppings:**
   Crumble blue cheese on top or drizzle with a bit of blue cheese dressing. Add a tiny celery stick or scallion for crunch and visual flair.

Serving Tip:

Serve cold or slightly chilled. For extra drama, add a drizzle of hot sauce just before serving and serve alongside celery sticks or carrot curls.

Buffalo Deviled Eggs – Ranch Version. Add your own level of heat with extra Buffalo wing sauce.

Buffalo Deviled Eggs – Ranch Version

This version swaps the bold blue cheese for a **cool and creamy ranch profile**, making it perfect for wing-lovers who like their heat with a soft landing. It's still spicy, still craveable—but smoothed out with herby, garlicky ranch goodness.

Ingredients:

- 12 large eggs
- 1/3 cup mayonnaise
- 1 tbsp hot sauce (Frank's RedHot recommended)
- 1 tbsp ranch dressing (or 1 tsp dry ranch seasoning + 1 tbsp sour cream)
- 1 tsp white vinegar or lemon juice
- 2 tbsp finely shredded cooked chicken breast
- Salt and pepper to taste

Optional Garnish:

- Celery slivers
- A drizzle of ranch dressing
- A few dots of hot sauce

- Minced fresh parsley or chives

Instructions:

1. **Boil and Peel the Eggs:**
   Hard boil for 10–12 minutes, cool in an ice bath, peel gently.

2. **Prepare the Filling:**
   Mash yolks with mayo, hot sauce, ranch dressing, and vinegar until smooth. Fold in finely shredded chicken. Add salt and pepper to taste.

3. **Assemble:**
   Pipe or spoon the creamy, zesty filling into the egg whites.

4. **Garnish:**
   Top with a celery sliver and a light drizzle of ranch or hot sauce. Add a sprinkle of parsley or chives for a pop of green.

Why This Version Rocks:

It's got the heat of Buffalo wings, the cool of ranch dip, and the familiarity of your favorite game day snack—all in one polished, party-perfect bite.

Burlington Maple & Cheddar Deviled Eggs

Burlington Maple & Cheddar Deviled Eggs

Sweet, sharp, and perfectly balanced—like Vermont in a bite. Deviled eggs filled with creamy yolk mixture blended with pure maple syrup and shredded sharp Vermont cheddar. Each is garnished with a drizzle of maple syrup and sprinkled with cheddar crumbs.

Why It's Uniquely Burlington:

Vermont is famous for its pure maple syrup and sharp cheddar cheese. This deviled egg blends creamy yolks with a touch of sweet maple and tangy cheddar, creating a harmonious flavor that celebrates Burlington's artisanal food culture.

Ingredients:

- 12 large eggs
- 1/4 cup mayonnaise
- 1 tbsp pure maple syrup
- 1/4 cup shredded sharp Vermont cheddar
- Salt and pepper to taste

Garnish:

- Tiny drizzle of maple syrup
- Shaved cheddar or cheddar crumbs

- Optional: sprinkle of cracked black pepper or fresh thyme

Instructions:

1. **Boil and Cool the Eggs:**
   Standard: boil, rest, ice bath, peel.

2. **Make the Filling:**
   Mash yolks with mayo and maple syrup. Fold in cheddar and season to taste.

3. **Assemble the Eggs:**
   Pipe or spoon filling into whites.

4. **Garnish with Vermont Flair:**
   Drizzle with maple syrup, sprinkle cheddar, and add optional pepper or thyme.

Serving Vibe:

Serve on a rustic wooden board with autumn leaves or a cozy cabin vibe. Perfect for fall gatherings and farm-to-table brunches.

Charlotte Pimento Cheese & Pulled Pork Deviled Eggs

Charlotte Pimento Cheese & Pulled Pork Deviled Eggs

Creamy, smoky, and packed with Carolina soul. Deviled eggs filled with creamy yolk mixture blended with pimento cheese and finely shredded pulled pork. Each egg is topped with a small pull of pork and sprinkled with paprika or cayenne.

Why It's Uniquely Charlotte:

Charlotte's food scene celebrates classic Southern flavors with a modern twist. This deviled egg combines the creamy tang of pimento cheese with tender pulled pork, embodying the city's barbecue passion and rich culinary heritage.

Ingredients:

- 12 large eggs
- 1/3 cup mayonnaise
- 1/4 cup pimento cheese
- 1/3 cup finely shredded pulled pork (smoked or slow-cooked)
- 1 tsp apple cider vinegar (optional, for tang)
- Salt and pepper to taste

Topping:

- Pulled pork shred
- Paprika or cayenne sprinkle
- Optional: fresh parsley or chives

Instructions:

1. **Boil and Cool the Eggs:**
   Standard boil, ice bath, peel.

2. **Make the Filling:**
   Mash yolks with mayo, pimento cheese, pulled pork, and vinegar. Season well.

3. **Assemble the Eggs:**
   Pipe or spoon filling into whites.

4. **Garnish with Carolina Flair:**
   Top with pulled pork and sprinkle paprika or cayenne.

Serving Vibe:

Serve on a wooden board with sweet tea or local craft beer. Perfect for backyard cookouts, game days, or Southern gatherings.

Charlottesville Goat Cheese & Fig Deviled Eggs

Charlottesville Goat Cheese & Fig Deviled Eggs

Creamy, sweet, and elegantly rustic. Deviled eggs filled with creamy yolk mixture blended with softened goat cheese and sweet fig preserves. Each egg is garnished with a small dollop of fig preserves, crumbled goat cheese, and fresh thyme or microgreens.

Why It's Uniquely Charlottesville:

Charlottesville is famous for its artisanal cheeses and vineyards. This deviled egg blends tangy local goat cheese with sweet fig preserves, creating a sophisticated balance of creamy and fruity flavors that reflect the region's farm-to-table ethos.

Ingredients:

- 12 large eggs
- 1/3 cup mayonnaise
- 2 tbsp local goat cheese, softened
- 1 tbsp fig preserves
- 1 tsp lemon juice
- Salt and pepper to taste

Garnish:

- Small slice or dollop of fig preserves
- Crumbled goat cheese

- Fresh thyme or microgreens

Instructions:

1. **Boil and Cool the Eggs:**
   Standard boil, ice bath, peel.

2. **Make the Filling:**
   Mash yolks with mayo, goat cheese, fig preserves, and lemon juice. Season to taste.

3. **Assemble the Eggs:**
   Pipe or spoon filling into whites.

4. **Garnish with Vineyard Elegance:**
   Top with fig preserves, crumbled goat cheese, and fresh herbs.

Serving Vibe:

Serve on a rustic wooden board with local Virginia wines and fresh bread. Perfect for vineyard tastings or elegant garden parties.

Charleston, SC Shrimp & Grits Deviled Eggs

Charleston, SC Shrimp & Grits Deviled Eggs

Creamy, spicy, and comfortingly elegant. filled with creamy yolk mixture blended with shredded sharp cheddar and a hint of hot sauce or Creole seasoning. Each egg is topped with a small cooked shrimp, a sprinkle of smoked paprika, and chopped parsley or chives.

Why It's Uniquely Charleston:

Shrimp and grits is a Lowcountry classic—simple yet luxurious. This deviled egg captures those flavors with creamy yolks mixed with a touch of cheddar and a hint of spice, topped with a small shrimp and a sprinkle of smoked paprika. It's Southern hospitality in one perfect bite.

Ingredients:

- 12 large eggs
- 1/4 cup mayonnaise
- 2 tbsp shredded sharp cheddar
- 1 tsp hot sauce or Creole seasoning
- 1 tsp lemon juice
- Salt and pepper to taste

Topping:

- Small cooked shrimp
- Smoked paprika
- Chopped parsley or chives

Instructions:

1. **Boil and Cool the Eggs:**
   Standard boil, ice bath, peel.

2. **Make the Filling:**
   Mash yolks with mayo, cheddar, hot sauce, and lemon juice. Season to taste.

3. **Assemble the Eggs:**
   Pipe or spoon filling into whites.

4. **Garnish with Lowcountry Flair:**
   Top with a small shrimp, sprinkle smoked paprika, and fresh herbs.

Serving Vibe:

Serve on a rustic wooden board with mint juleps or sweet tea. Perfect for porch parties or elegant Southern gatherings.

Charleston, WV:. Pepperoni & sauerkraut Deviled Eggs

Charleston, WV Pepperoni & Sauerkraut Deviled Eggs

Savory, tangy, and with a smoky Appalachian twist. Deviled eggs filled with creamy yolk mixture blended with diced pepperoni and finely chopped sauerkraut. Each egg is topped with a sprinkle of smoked paprika and a small crisp slice of pepperoni

Why It's Uniquely Charleston:

West Virginia cuisine reflects its Appalachian heritage—simple, hearty, and full of bold flavors. This deviled egg combines creamy yolks with diced pepperoni and tangy sauerkraut, topped with a sprinkle of smoked paprika for a smoky finish. It's a unique blend of comfort and spice.

Ingredients:

- 12 large eggs
- 1/3 cup mayonnaise
- 1 tbsp Dijon mustard
- 2 tbsp diced pepperoni
- 1 tbsp finely chopped sauerkraut, drained
- Salt and pepper to taste

Topping:

- Smoked paprika
- Small pepperoni slice or crisp
- Optional: chopped fresh parsley

Instructions:

1. **Boil and Cool the Eggs:**
   Standard method: boil, rest, ice bath, peel.

2. **Make the Filling:**
   Mash yolks with mayo, mustard, pepperoni, and sauerkraut. Season well.

3. **Assemble the Eggs:**
   Pipe or spoon filling into whites.

4. **Garnish with Appalachian Flair:**
   Top with smoked paprika, a small pepperoni crisp, and fresh herbs.

Serving Vibe:

Serve on a rustic wooden board with local craft beer or cider. Perfect for Appalachian gatherings or hearty game days.

Cheyenne Bison & Sweet Onion deviled Eggs

Cheyenne Bison & Sweet Onion Deviled Eggs

Smoky, savory, and with a touch of sweet Western charm. Deviled eggs filled with creamy yolk mixture blended with cooked ground bison and caramelized sweet onions. Each egg is topped with a small, caramelized onion curl and sprinkled with smoked paprika or fresh thyme

---

Why It's Uniquely Cheyenne:

Wyoming's cuisine is defined by its game meats and straightforward, bold flavors. This deviled egg combines creamy yolks with smoky ground bison and a hint of caramelized sweet onions, offering a bite that's both rustic and refined.

Ingredients:

- 12 large eggs
- 1/3 cup mayonnaise
- 1 tbsp Dijon mustard
- 2 tbsp cooked ground bison (or lean beef)
- 2 tbsp caramelized sweet onions
- Salt and pepper to taste

Topping:

- Small caramelized onion curl or crisp
- Sprinkle of smoked paprika or fresh thyme

Instructions:

1. **Boil and Cool the Eggs:**
   Standard method: boil, rest, ice bath, peel.

2. **Make the Filling:**
   Mash yolks with mayo, mustard, bison, and caramelized onions. Season well.

3. **Assemble the Eggs:**
   Pipe or spoon filling into egg whites.

4. **Garnish with Western Flair:**
   Top with a caramelized onion curl and sprinkle smoked paprika or thyme.

Serving Vibe:

Serve on a rustic wooden board with craft beer or Wyoming whiskey. Perfect for cowboy cookouts or Western-themed gatherings.

Chicago Giardiniera & Salami Deviled Eggs

Chicago Giardiniera & Salami Deviled Eggs

Tangy, meaty, and straight from the deli counter of the Windy City. Deviled eggs with a creamy yellow filling flecked with colorful chopped giardiniera (carrots, peppers, cauliflower). Each egg is topped with a thin slice or cube of dry salami or Italian beef.

Why It's Uniquely Chicago:

Forget deep-dish pizza for a sec—Chicago is also known for **Italian beef sandwiches**, loaded with **giardiniera** (that crunchy, spicy pickled vegetable mix), and iconic **South Side delis**. This deviled egg captures those bold, briny, beefy vibes: chopped giardiniera stirred into the yolk, a sliver of salami or beef on top. Street food meets speakeasy chic.

Ingredients:

- 12 large eggs
- 1/3 cup mayonnaise
- 1 tsp yellow mustard or Dijon
- 1 tbsp finely chopped **giardiniera** (drained)
- Salt and black pepper to taste

Topping Options:

- Thin strip or cube of **dry salami**, **capicola**, or **Italian beef**

- Extra giardiniera bits
- Optional parsley or shaved Parm for garnish

Instructions:

1. **Boil and Cool the Eggs:**
   Classic method: boil, rest, ice bath, peel.

2. **Make the Filling:**
   Mash yolks with mayo, mustard, and finely chopped giardiniera. Adjust seasoning.

3. **Assemble the Eggs:**
   Pipe or spoon into whites.

4. **Top It Off:**
   Add a small piece of salami or capicola, a garnish of giardiniera or herbs, and serve with swagger.

Serving Vibe:

Serve on a black slate tray or metal dish, surrounded by deli paper, sport peppers, or even mini toothpicks with Chicago flags.

Cincinnati 5-Way Chili Deviled Eggs

Cincinnati 5-Way Chili Deviled Eggs

Savory, spicy, and layered with classic Cincinnati flavors. Deviled eggs filled with creamy yolk mixed with spiced Cincinnati-style chili, piped into egg whites. Each egg is topped with finely diced onions, a spoonful of chili beans, shredded cheddar cheese, and a light dusting of chili powder

Why It's Uniquely Cincinnati:

The 5-way chili is a beloved Cincinnati specialty: spaghetti topped with chili, beans, onions, and shredded cheese. This deviled egg distills that rich, hearty flavor into a creamy yolk mixed with chili spices, topped with diced onions, beans, and cheddar for a perfect bite of Cincinnati tradition.

Ingredients:

- 12 large eggs
- 1/3 cup mayonnaise
- 1 tbsp prepared Cincinnati-style chili or homemade chili with cinnamon and spices
- 1 tsp yellow mustard
- Salt and pepper to taste

Toppings:

- Finely diced onions
- Small spoonful of kidney or chili beans
- Shredded cheddar cheese
- Optional: dash of chili powder or hot sauce

Instructions:

1. **Boil and Cool the Eggs:**
   Standard: boil, rest, ice bath, peel.

2. **Make the Filling:**
   Mash yolks with mayo, chili, and mustard. Season to taste.

3. **Assemble the Eggs:**
   Pipe or spoon filling into whites.

4. **Top with 5-Way Fixings:**
   Add diced onions, chili beans, shredded cheddar, and optional chili powder.

🍴 Serving Vibe:

Serve on a casual tray with napkins printed like chili parlors, perfect for game day or a casual get-together with friends.

D.C. Embassy Row Deviled Eggs with Sumac & Tahini

D.C. Embassy Row Deviled Eggs with Sumac & Tahini

Global, refined, and worthy of a state dinner.

Why It's Uniquely D.C.:

Washington, D.C. is a true global crossroads—embassies line the streets, cuisines from every continent fill the neighborhoods, and diplomacy is on the daily menu. This deviled egg reflects that rich mix: **creamy yolks blended with tahini and lemon**, topped with a sprinkle of **sumac** for tang and color. It's refined, worldly, and packed with flavor—like the best of D.C.

Ingredients:

- 12 large eggs
- 1/3 cup mayonnaise
- 1 tbsp **tahini**
- 1 tsp lemon juice
- 1/4 tsp garlic powder
- Salt and pepper to taste

Garnish:

- Sprinkle of **sumac**
- Tiny parsley leaf or edible flower petal

- Optional: a chickpea or olive sliver

Instructions:

1. **Boil and Cool the Eggs:**
   - Boil, rest, ice bath, peel.
2. **Make the Filling:**
   - Halve eggs, remove yolks.
   - Mash with mayo, tahini, lemon juice, and garlic powder.
   - Mix until smooth. Season with salt and pepper.
3. **Assemble the Eggs:**
   - Pipe or spoon into whites.
4. **Garnish Like a Diplomat:**
   - Sprinkle with sumac and top with a delicate leaf or garnish of choice.

Serving Vibe:

Serve on fine china or a sleek black slate tray with gold cocktail forks and a glass of Champagne or mint tea—perfect for a rooftop reception or late-night poli

Detroit Coney Island Chili & Cheese Deviled Eggs

Detroit Coney Island Chili & Cheese Deviled Eggs

Savory, cheesy, and packed with classic Motor City flavors. Deviled eggs filled with creamy yolk mixed with chili and mustard, topped with shredded sharp cheddar and diced white onions.

Why It's Uniquely Detroit:

Detroit's Coney Island hot dogs are a city institution, topped with chili, onions, and mustard. This deviled egg reinvents that experience, mixing savory chili spices into the yolk and topping it with shredded cheddar and diced onions. It's a bite-sized ode to Detroit's heart and hustle.

Ingredients:

- 12 large eggs
- 1/3 cup mayonnaise
- 1 tsp yellow mustard
- 1/3 cup prepared chili (no beans, seasoned)
- 1/4 cup shredded sharp cheddar cheese
- 2 tbsp finely diced onions (white or yellow)
- Salt and black pepper to taste

Toppings:

- Extra cheddar
- Diced onions
- Optional: a tiny dash of chili powder or hot sauce

Instructions:

1. **Boil and Cool the Eggs:**
   Classic: boil, ice bath, peel.

2. **Make the Filling:**
   Mash yolks with mayo, mustard, and a few spoonfuls of chili until creamy but textured. Season to taste.

3. **Assemble the Eggs:**
   Pipe or spoon the chili-infused yolk into whites.

4. **Top It Off:**
   Garnish with shredded cheddar, diced onions, and an optional sprinkle of chili powder.

Serving Vibe:

Serve on a retro diner-style platter or vintage enamel tray with a side of Detroit jazz or Motown vinyl spinning. Perfect for game day or a city street party.

Denver Green Chili & Cheddar Deviled Eggs

Denver Green Chili & Cheddar Deviled Eggs

Spicy, cheesy, and mile-high flavor. A deviled egg filled with a pale yellow and green speckled mixture of cheddar and roasted green chiles, topped with a shaved cheddar curl and a dusting of smoked paprika.

Why It's Uniquely Colorado:

Colorado cuisine often means bold comfort with a fresh twist—think green chiles from Pueblo, artisanal cheeses, and hearty brunches after mountain hikes. This deviled egg features **roasted green chiles** (mild or hot), **sharp white cheddar**, and a hint of **smoked paprika**. It's spicy enough to be fun and savory enough to make it disappear fast.

Ingredients:

- 12 large eggs
- 1/3 cup mayonnaise
- 1 tsp Dijon mustard
- 1–2 tbsp finely chopped **roasted green chiles** (like Pueblo or Hatch)
- 1/4 cup **shredded sharp white cheddar**
- 1/4 tsp smoked paprika
- Salt and pepper to taste

Optional Garnish:

- Shaved cheddar curl
- Dusting of paprika
- Sliver of chile or chopped chive

Instructions:

1. **Boil and Cool the Eggs:**
    - Standard method: boil, rest, ice bath, peel.
2. **Make the Filling:**
    - Halve eggs and remove yolks.
    - Mash yolks with mayo, mustard, chopped green chile, and cheddar.
    - Mix until smooth or slightly textured. Add paprika, salt, and pepper.
3. **Assemble the Eggs:**
    - Pipe or spoon filling into egg whites.
4. **Top with Mile-High Flavor:**
    - Garnish with shaved cheddar, a bit of chile, or smoked paprika dust.

Serving Vibe:

Perfect on a rustic wooden board at a cozy après-ski party—or for brunch in Boulder with kombucha and craft beer.

Des Moines Sweet Corn & Smoked Gouda Deviled Eggs

Des Moines Sweet Corn & Smoked Gouda Deviled Eggs

Creamy, smoky, and Iowa proud—with a market-fresh bite. Deviled eggs filled with a creamy yellow mixture flecked with golden roasted corn and soft bits of smoked gouda. Each egg is topped with a charred corn kernel, shaved gouda, or tiny microgreen.

Why It's Uniquely Des Moines:

Sweet corn is Iowa's pride—and Des Moines blends farm-fresh ingredients with a growing foodie scene. We elevate the deviled egg by folding in roasted sweet corn and smoked gouda for a creamy-sweet, slightly smoky filling. It's farmers' market meets wine bar.

Ingredients:

- 12 large eggs
- 1/3 cup mayonnaise
- 1 tsp Dijon mustard
- 1/4 cup **roasted or grilled corn kernels** (cut from cob or frozen, thawed)
- 2 tbsp shredded or finely chopped **smoked gouda**
- Salt and pepper to taste

Optional Garnishes:

- Charred corn kernel or shaved gouda

- Paprika or chive sprig
- Tiny microgreen

Instructions:

1. **Boil and Cool the Eggs:**
   Standard: boil, rest, ice bath, peel.

2. **Make the Filling:**
   Mash yolks with mayo and mustard. Fold in roasted corn and gouda. Blend until creamy with some texture. Season with salt and pepper.

3. **Assemble the Eggs:**
   Pipe or spoon into whites.

4. **Garnish Des Moines Style:**
   Top with a golden corn kernel, gouda shaving, or chive/microgreen for that classy touch.

Serving Vibe:

Serve on a stoneware plate with modern farm-to-table aesthetic—think reclaimed wood, ceramic dishes, and fresh herbs nearby. Perfect for wine night, brunch, or upscale tailgate.

Fargo Wild Mushroom & Caraway Deviled Eggs

Earthy, aromatic, and deeply comforting. Deviled eggs filled with creamy yolk mixture blended with finely chopped sautéed wild mushrooms and flecked with ground caraway seeds. Each egg is topped with a small sautéed mushroom slice and a sprinkle of caraway seeds or fresh parsley.

Why It's Uniquely Fargo:

North Dakota's landscape is dotted with wild mushrooms and has strong Eastern European influences where caraway is a beloved spice. This deviled egg blends sautéed wild mushrooms, creamy yolks, and a hint of caraway seed for a warm, woodsy flavor—perfect for a city balancing rugged plains and cultural richness.

Ingredients:

- 12 large eggs
- 1/3 cup mayonnaise
- 1/4 cup finely chopped sautéed wild mushrooms (shiitake, cremini, or chanterelle)
- 1/2 tsp ground caraway seeds (or crushed whole)
- Salt and pepper to taste

Garnish:

- Tiny sautéed mushroom slice

- Sprinkle of caraway seeds or fresh parsley

Instructions:

1. **Boil and Cool the Eggs:**
   Standard boil, ice bath, peel.

2. **Make the Filling:**
   Mash yolks with mayo, sautéed mushrooms, and caraway. Season to taste.

3. **Assemble the Eggs:**
   Pipe or spoon filling into egg whites.

4. **Garnish with Earthy Flair:**
   Top with a tiny mushroom slice and sprinkle caraway or parsley.

Serving Vibe:

Serve on a rustic wood board or stoneware with forest-themed décor—pinecones, moss, and warm candlelight for cozy North Dakota nights.

Galveston Tuna Salad Deviled Eggs

Galveston Tuna Salad Deviled Eggs

Fresh, creamy, and packed with coastal flavor. Deviled eggs filled with creamy yolk mixture blended with flaky tuna, finely chopped celery, lemon juice, and fresh herbs. Each egg is garnished with a small celery leaf or dill sprig and a light sprinkle of lemon zest.

Why It's Uniquely Portland:

Portland's vibrant seafood scene means fresh, well-made tuna salad is a local favorite. This deviled egg blends creamy yolks with flaky tuna, crisp celery, and fresh herbs for a refreshing and satisfying bite.

Ingredients:

- 12 large eggs
- 1/3 cup mayonnaise
- 1/2 cup canned tuna (preferably packed in water), drained and flaked
- 2 tbsp finely chopped celery
- 1 tbsp chopped fresh dill or parsley
- 1 tsp lemon juice
- Salt and pepper to taste

Garnish:

- Small celery leaf or fresh dill sprig
- Optional: lemon zest

Instructions:

1. **Boil and Cool the Eggs:**
   Standard boil, ice bath, peel.

2. **Make the Filling:**
   Mash yolks with mayo, lemon juice, and herbs. Fold in tuna and celery. Season to taste.

3. **Assemble the Eggs:**
   Pipe or spoon filling into whites.

4. **Garnish with Coastal Freshness:**
   Top with a celery leaf or dill sprig and optional lemon zest.

Serving Vibe:

Serve on a crisp white plate with nautical décor and a glass of chilled white wine or local craft beer. Perfect for seaside brunches or summer gatherings.

Hilton Head Crab & Cajun Deviled Eggs

Hilton Head Crab & Cajun Deviled Eggs

Spicy, creamy, and bursting with coastal zest. Deviled eggs filled with creamy yolk mixture blended with fresh lump crab meat and Cajun seasoning. Each egg is topped with a sprinkle of smoked paprika and chopped green onions, with an optional drizzle of hot sauce.

Why It's Uniquely Hilton Head:

Hilton Head's coastal cuisine is rich with fresh seafood and Cajun spices. This deviled egg blends creamy yolks with fresh crab meat and a kick of Cajun seasoning, topped with a dash of smoked paprika and chopped green onions for a vibrant finish.

Ingredients:

- 12 large eggs
- 1/3 cup mayonnaise
- 2 tbsp lump crab meat, picked over shells
- 1 tsp Cajun seasoning
- 1 tsp Dijon mustard
- Salt and pepper to taste

Garnish:

- Sprinkle of smoked paprika

- Chopped green onions
- Optional: a tiny drizzle of hot sauce

Instructions:

1. **Boil and Cool the Eggs:**
   Standard boil, rest, ice bath, peel.

2. **Make the Filling:**
   Mash yolks with mayo, mustard, Cajun seasoning, and crab meat. Season to taste.

3. **Assemble the Eggs:**
   Pipe or spoon filling into whites.

4. **Garnish with Island Spice:**
   Sprinkle paprika, green onions, and optional hot sauce drizzle.

Serving Vibe:

Serve on a coastal-themed platter with beachy décor and chilled white wine or fruity cocktails. Perfect for summer parties or seaside dinners.

Honolulu spam Musubi Deviled Eggs

Honolulu Spam Musubi Deviled Eggs

Savory, sweet, and totally ono. A deviled egg with creamy, pale yellow filling, topped with a glazed cube or strip of Spam and a sprinkle of furikake or sesame seeds. Optional thin nori strip for a nod to sushi.

Why It's Uniquely Honolulu:

Spam musubi is a Hawaiian classic—grilled Spam, sticky rice, and seaweed, often found in lunchboxes and gas station counters alike. This deviled egg borrows that flavor combo: sweet-savory glaze, a touch of soy, and a crispy Spam topper. It's urban island soul in one silky bite.

Ingredients:

- 12 large eggs
- 1/3 cup mayonnaise
- 1 tsp soy sauce
- 1/2 tsp rice vinegar or mirin
- 1/4 tsp sugar or honey (for balance)
- Salt and pepper to taste

Topping:

- Tiny cube or strip of **pan-fried Spam**, glazed with soy sauce + sugar

- Optional: sprinkle of **furikake** or sesame seeds
- Optional: thin nori strip for visual flair

Instructions:

1. **Boil and Cool the Eggs:**
   Standard: boil, rest, ice bath, peel.

2. **Make the Filling:**
   Halve eggs, mash yolks with mayo, soy sauce, vinegar/mirin, and sugar. Adjust seasoning.

3. **Assemble the Eggs:**
   Pipe or spoon into whites.

4. **Garnish Island Style:**
   Top with glazed Spam piece, furikake, and optional nori strip.

Serving Vibe:

Serve on a bamboo platter with a plumeria flower nearby, or on black slate with chopsticks and a tropical cocktail—perfect for a backyard luau or beach city brunch.

Indianapolis Cornbread & Jalapeno Deviled Eggs

Indianapolis Cornbread & Jalapeño Deviled Eggs

Warm, buttery, and just a little bit spicy—like race day with a Southern twist. Deviled eggs with creamy filling flecked with yellow cornmeal and tiny green jalapeño pieces. Each egg is topped with toasted cornbread crumble and a thin slice of pickled or fresh jalapeño.

Why It's Uniquely Indianapolis:

In Indy, you've got race cars, tailgate traditions, and Midwestern hospitality in every bite. This deviled egg takes inspiration from classic **cornbread and jalapeño muffins**—a staple at potlucks and backyard barbecues across the state. We infuse the yolk with a hint of cornmeal butteriness and top it with a sprinkle of cornbread crumble and a tiny slice of pickled jalapeño.

Ingredients:

- 12 large eggs
- 1/4 cup mayonnaise
- 1 tsp yellow mustard
- 1 tsp finely ground cornmeal (optional, for texture)
- 1/2 tsp melted butter
- Salt and pepper to taste

Mix-Ins:

- 1 tsp finely chopped pickled jalapeño

- Optional: a dash of honey for sweet heat balance

Topping:

- Cornbread crumble (toasted or baked crisp)
- Thin slice of pickled or fresh jalapeño
- Optional: tiny cilantro leaf or micro basil

Instructions:

1. **Boil and Cool the Eggs:**
   Standard: boil, rest, ice bath, peel.

2. **Make the Filling:**
   Mash yolks with mayo, mustard, butter, and cornmeal (if using). Stir in chopped jalapeño. Season to taste.

3. **Assemble the Eggs:**
   Pipe or spoon filling into whites.

4. **Garnish with Speedway Flair:**
   Top with crispy cornbread crumble and a jalapeño slice.

Serving Vibe:

Perfect for race day spreads, brewery bites, or backyard firepit hangs. Serve on a rustic wood board or race-checkered napkins.

Jackso BBQ & Pickled Jalapeno Deviled Eggs

Jackson BBQ & Pickled Jalapeño Deviled Eggs

Smoky, tangy, and with a spicy kick that sings the Delta blues. Deviled eggs filled with creamy, golden yolk mixed with smoky barbecue sauce and a hint of mustard. Each egg is topped with thin slices of pickled jalapeño and a dusting of smoked paprika or cayenne.

Why It's Uniquely Jackson:

Jackson is steeped in blues music, smoky barbecue joints, and bold Southern flavors. This deviled egg reflects that vibe with a creamy yolk filling enhanced by smoky barbecue sauce and topped with tangy, spicy pickled jalapeños. It's a bite that dances on your tongue.

Ingredients:

- 12 large eggs
- 1/3 cup mayonnaise
- 1 tsp yellow mustard
- 1 tbsp smoky barbecue sauce (your favorite)
- Salt and black pepper to taste

Topping:

- Thin slices of pickled jalapeño
- Optional: dash of smoked paprika or cayenne

Instructions:

1. **Boil and Cool the Eggs:**
   Standard: boil, rest, ice bath, peel.

2. **Make the Filling:**
   Mash yolks with mayo, mustard, and barbecue sauce. Season to taste.

3. **Assemble the Eggs:**
   Pipe or spoon filling into egg whites.

4. **Garnish with Delta Flavor:**
   Top with pickled jalapeño slices and a sprinkle of smoked paprika.

Serving Vibe:

Serve with sweet, iced tea, cornbread, and some blues music in the background for the full Jackson experience.

Kansas City BBQ Deviled Eggs

Kansas City BBQ Deviled Eggs

This one's bold, smoky, sweet, and tangy—**deviled eggs with BBQ sauce and pulled beef or brisket**, just like you'd find at a Wichita cookout or a Kansas City tailgate.

Ingredients:

- 12 large eggs
- 1/3 cup mayonnaise
- 1 tbsp Kansas City–style BBQ sauce (thick, sweet, smoky)
- 1 tsp yellow or Dijon mustard
- 1/4 tsp smoked paprika
- Salt and pepper to taste
- Optional: 2–3 tbsp finely chopped smoked brisket, pulled beef, or BBQ chicken
- Garnish: extra BBQ drizzle, chives, or a sliver of smoked meat

Instructions:

1. **Boil and Cool Eggs:**
   Boil, chill in an ice bath, peel.

2. **Make the Filling:**
   Mash yolks with mayo, BBQ sauce, mustard, and smoked paprika. Fold in chopped smoked meat if using. Add salt and pepper to taste.

3. **Assemble:**
   Pipe or spoon filling into egg whites.

4. **Garnish:**
   Drizzle with more BBQ sauce, a sliver of meat, or chopped chives. A sprinkle of fried onion bits also works great.

Why It's Uniquely Kansas:

Kansas loves its **low and slow BBQ**, and this deviled egg brings those **rich, smoky, saucy flavors** to the potluck table. It's basically a brisket sandwich and deviled egg all in one.

Key West Lime & Cilantro Deviled Eggs

Key West Lime & Cilantro Deviled Eggs

These deviled eggs are cool, creamy, and kissed with citrus and herbs—perfect for a beachside brunch or Miami garden party.

Why It's Uniquely Florida:

Florida is the **home of the Key lime** and has a **strong Caribbean and Latin influence**, especially in places like Miami and Tampa. This recipe brings the brightness of the tropics and the freshness of the coast straight into your deviled eggs.

Ingredients:

- 12 large eggs
- 1/3 cup mayonnaise
- 1 tbsp fresh Key lime juice (or regular lime if unavailable)
- 1/2 tsp Dijon mustard
- 1/2 tsp honey or agave (optional, for balance)
- 1 tbsp finely chopped fresh cilantro
- Salt and pepper to taste
- Optional: a pinch of zest from the Key lime

- Garnish: lime zest, cilantro leaf, or a tiny sliver of sweet pepper

---

Instructions:

1. **Boil and Cool the Eggs:**
   Standard method: boil, rest, ice bath, peel.

2. **Prepare the Filling:**
   Halve the eggs, remove yolks. Mash yolks with mayo, lime juice, mustard, honey (if using), and chopped cilantro. Mix until smooth. Add salt and pepper to taste.

3. **Assemble the Eggs:**
   Pipe or spoon mixture into whites. Chill until ready to serve.

4. **Garnish:**
   Top with lime zest and a cilantro leaf or a colorful sliver of sweet pepper for a tropical pop.

Las Vegas Bacon-Wrapped Dates & Manchego Deviled Eggs

Las Vegas Bacon-Wrapped Dates & Manchego Deviled Eggs

Sweet, smoky, and a little bit decadent—like Vegas nightlife in a bite.

Deviled eggs filled with creamy yolk mixed with finely chopped bacon-wrapped dates and shredded Manchego cheese. Each egg is topped with a small piece of bacon-wrapped date and a shaving of Manchego.

Why It's Uniquely Vegas:

Vegas is the place where indulgence meets culinary creativity. These deviled eggs combine creamy yolks with the sweet-savory combo of **bacon-wrapped dates**, enhanced with sharp **Manchego cheese**. It's flashy, fun, and perfect for a high-energy party.

Ingredients:

- 12 large eggs
- 1/3 cup mayonnaise
- 1 tsp Dijon mustard
- 2 tbsp finely chopped **bacon-wrapped dates** (cooked, pitted dates wrapped in bacon and chopped)
- 2 tbsp shredded Manchego cheese
- Salt and pepper to taste

Topping:

- Small piece of bacon-wrapped date
- Shaved Manchego
- Optional: drizzle of balsamic reduction or honey

Instructions:

1. **Boil and Cool the Eggs:**
   Standard: boil, ice bath, peel.

2. **Make the Filling:**
   Mash yolks with mayo, mustard, chopped bacon-wrapped dates, and Manchego. Season to taste.

3. **Assemble the Eggs:**
   Pipe or spoon into whites.

4. **Garnish Vegas Style:**
   Top with a small piece of bacon-wrapped date, Manchego shaving, and optional drizzle.

Serving Vibe:

Serve on a glossy black or mirrored platter with cocktail picks and vibrant lighting. Perfect for casino parties, rooftop bars, or a night out on the Strip.

Lawrence Roasted Beet & Herbed Goat Cheese Deviled Eggs

Lawrence Roasted Beet & Herbed Goat Cheese Deviled Eggs

Vibrant, earthy, and unapologetically artsy. Deviled eggs with a vibrant pink filling from roasted beet and goat cheese, piped elegantly into egg whites. Each egg is topped with crumbled goat cheese, a sprig of dill or chive, or a thin beet ribbon

Why It's Uniquely Lawrence:

Lawrence is full of indie coffeehouses, art galleries, and creative energy—where food is as colorful as the street murals. This deviled egg features a striking beet-pink filling swirled with tangy goat cheese and fresh herbs. It's modern, vegetarian-friendly, and unforgettable.

Ingredients:

- 12 large eggs
- 1/4 cup mayonnaise
- 2 oz **herbed goat cheese**, softened
- 1/4 cup **roasted beets**, finely grated or pureed
- 1 tsp lemon juice
- Salt and pepper to taste

Optional Garnish:

- Crumbled goat cheese

- Dill or chive sprig
- Thin beet ribbon or microgreens

Instructions:

1. **Boil and Cool the Eggs:**
   Standard method: boil, rest, ice bath, peel.

2. **Make the Filling:**
   Mash yolks with mayo, beet puree, and goat cheese until creamy and vibrantly pink. Add lemon juice, salt, and pepper to balance the tang and earthiness.

3. **Assemble the Eggs:**
   Pipe or spoon the vivid filling into the whites.

4. **Garnish Like a Gallery Plate:**
   Add a crumble of goat cheese, a tiny dill sprig, or a beet ribbon. Make it artsy.

Serving Vibe:

Serve on a slate or terrazzo plate with bright cloth napkins or abstract ceramic dishes. Perfect for poetry nights, rooftop parties, or vegan-forward brunches (just sub the mayo).

Little Rock Fried Pickle Deviled Eggs

Little Rock Fried Pickle Deviled Eggs

Crunchy, creamy, and unapologetically Southern. A deviled egg filled with creamy, golden yolk speckled with dill and topped with a small, crispy fried pickle slice.

Why It's Uniquely Arkansas:

Fried pickles were born in Arkansas, and they're now a staple in bars and backyard cookouts alike. This deviled egg is inspired by that iconic snack: **tangy pickle juice in the filling, topped with a crispy fried pickle chip or breaded garnish.** Bold, briny, and full of charm—like Arkansas itself.

Ingredients:

- 12 large eggs
- 1/3 cup mayonnaise
- 1 tsp yellow mustard
- 2 tsp dill pickle juice
- 1 tsp finely chopped pickles
- Salt and pepper to taste

Topping:

- **Mini fried pickle slice** *(use a small dill chip, breaded and fried)*

- Optional: sprinkle of smoked paprika or hot sauce dot

Optional:

- Pinch of garlic powder in the yolk mix
- Chopped fresh dill

Instructions:

1. **Boil and Cool the Eggs:**
    - Standard boil, ice bath, peel.
2. **Make the Filling:**
    - Slice eggs and remove yolks.
    - Mash yolks with mayo, mustard, pickle juice, and chopped pickles.
    - Season with salt, pepper, and a pinch of garlic powder if desired.
3. **Assemble the Eggs:**
    - Pipe or spoon filling into whites.
4. **Top It Off:**
    - Add one **crispy fried pickle chip** on top of each egg.
    - Optional: sprinkle with paprika or add a tiny hot sauce dot.

Serving Vibe:

Serve with sweet tea or beer, bluegrass on the speakers, and your favorite vintage enamel plate.

Los Angeles Avocado & Sriracha Deviled Eggs

Los Angeles Avocado & Sriracha Deviled Eggs

Trendy, creamy, and totally Instagrammable. A deviled egg with bright green avocado filling swirled into the center, drizzled with Sriracha and sprinkled with black sesame seeds. Topped with a few delicate microgreens or a thin radish slice.

Why It's Uniquely L.A.:

L.A. is all about fusion, freshness, and flair. This deviled egg blends **rich avocado** with classic yolk, kicks it up with **Sriracha**, and finishes with a pop of **black sesame or microgreens**. Think: brunch in Silver Lake, wellness at Runyon Canyon, and just enough spice to keep it interesting.

Ingredients:

- 12 large eggs
- 1 ripe avocado
- 1/4 cup mayonnaise
- 1 tsp lime juice
- 1 tsp Sriracha (adjust to taste)
- Salt and pepper to taste

Optional Enhancements:

- Pinch of garlic powder or onion powder

- Chopped cilantro or chives

Topping Ideas:
- Drizzle of extra Sriracha
- Black sesame seeds
- Microgreens or a cilantro leaf
- Thin radish slice for visual pop

Instructions:

1. **Boil and Cool the Eggs:**
   - Standard: boil, rest, ice bath, peel.
2. **Make the Filling:**
   - Halve eggs, remove yolks.
   - Mash yolks with avocado, mayo, lime juice, and Sriracha.
   - Season to taste and mix until smooth and vibrant green.
3. **Assemble the Eggs:**
   - Pipe or spoon into whites.
4. **Top with California Cool:**
   - Garnish with black sesame, microgreens, or a Sriracha drizzle.

Serving Vibe:

Serve on a minimalist white plate with gold forks and marble background. Maybe a side of green juice or a turmeric latte. It's all about the *aesthetic*.

Louisville Bourbon Bacon Deviled Eggs

Louisville Bourbon Bacon Deviled Eggs

Rich, smoky, and just a little boozy. Derby Day approved. Deviled eggs filled with a creamy golden yolk mixture, speckled with bits of bacon and a hint of brown sugar. Each egg is topped with crumbled bacon, a tiny mint leaf, or a light dusting of smoked paprika.

Why It's Uniquely Louisville:

This city is the birthplace of the **Louisville Slugger**, the host of the **Kentucky Derby**, and a proud steward of **bourbon culture**. This deviled egg delivers all that charm in one perfect bite: crispy bacon, a hint of brown sugar, and a splash of real bourbon folded into a creamy yolk. Elegant enough for a julep-sipping garden party, bold enough for a tailgate.

Ingredients:

- 12 large eggs
- 1/3 cup mayonnaise
- 1 tsp Dijon mustard
- 1 tsp Kentucky bourbon
- 1/2 tsp brown sugar
- 1 tbsp finely crumbled crispy bacon (plus more for garnish)
- Salt and pepper to taste

Optional Garnish:

- Crumbled bacon
- Micro mint leaf
- Dash of smoked paprika

Instructions:

1. **Boil and Cool the Eggs:**
   Standard: boil, rest, ice bath, peel.

2. **Make the Filling:**
   Mash yolks with mayo, mustard, bourbon, and brown sugar. Fold in crumbled bacon. Season to taste.

3. **Assemble the Eggs:**
   Pipe or spoon filling into whites.

4. **Garnish Derby Style:**
   Sprinkle with more bacon, a mint leaf, or a whisper of smoked paprika.

Serving Vibe:

Serve on a vintage tray or slate board next to a glass of bourbon or mint julep. Perfect for Derby parties, bourbon tastings, or backyard porch hangs with bluegrass in the air.

Milwaukee Butter Burger Deviled Eggs

Milwaukee Butter Burger Deviled Eggs

Buttery, savory, and decadently beefy—a mini burger experience in every bite. Deviled eggs filled with creamy yolk mixture blended with seasoned cooked ground beef, melted butter, Worcestershire sauce, and shredded sharp cheddar cheese. Each egg is topped with a small dill pickle slice and crispy fried onion bits, with optional tiny drizzles of mustard or ketchup.

Why It's Uniquely Milwaukee:

Milwaukee's butter burger is legendary for its juicy beef patty smothered in butter, often topped with melted cheese and classic condiments. This deviled egg captures those rich, savory flavors with a creamy yolk filling mixed with ground beef, a hint of melted butter flavor, and sharp cheese, topped with a small pickle slice or crispy onion for crunch.

Ingredients:

- 12 large eggs
- 1/3 cup mayonnaise
- 1/4 cup cooked ground beef (seasoned like a burger patty)
- 2 tbsp finely shredded sharp cheddar cheese
- 1 tbsp melted butter (cooled)
- 1 tsp Worcestershire sauce
- Salt and pepper to taste

Topping:

- Small dill pickle slice or relish
- Crispy fried onion bits or finely chopped raw onion
- Optional: tiny mustard or ketchup drizzle

Instructions:

1. **Boil and Cool the Eggs:**
   Standard: boil, rest, ice bath, peel.

2. **Prepare the Filling:**
   Mash yolks with mayo, melted butter, Worcestershire sauce, ground beef, and cheddar. Season to taste.

3. **Assemble the Eggs:**
   Pipe or spoon filling into whites.

4. **Garnish with Burger Flair:**
   Top with a pickle slice, crispy onion bits, and optional mustard or ketchup drizzle.

Serving Vibe:

Serve on a classic diner-style platter with a side of fries or a Milwaukee lager. Perfect for game day or a fun party appetizer with Midwestern charm.

Minneapolis Wild Rice & Maple-Glazed Bacon Deviled Eggs

Minneapolis Wild Rice & Maple-Glazed Bacon Deviled Eggs

Nutty, sweet, and smoky—Minnesota nice on a plate. Deviled eggs filled with creamy yolk mixture speckled with cooked wild rice and bits of maple-glazed bacon. Each egg is garnished with chopped bacon, a thin drizzle of maple syrup, and fresh chopped chives or thyme.

Why It's Uniquely Minneapolis:

Minnesota staples like wild rice and maple syrup combine with smoky bacon to create a deviled egg that's cozy and sophisticated. This egg highlights local ingredients and that famous Minnesota sweetness balanced by savory bites.

Ingredients:

- 12 large eggs
- 1/3 cup mayonnaise
- 1 tsp Dijon mustard
- 1 tbsp cooked wild rice (cooked and cooled)
- 1 tbsp finely chopped maple-glazed bacon (or regular bacon with a drizzle of maple syrup)
- 1 tsp pure maple syrup
- Salt and pepper to taste

Garnish:

- Extra chopped bacon
- Maple drizzle
- Chopped chives or fresh thyme

Instructions:

1. **Boil and Cool the Eggs:**
   Standard: boil, rest, ice bath, peel.

2. **Make the Filling:**
   Mash yolks with mayo, mustard, and maple syrup. Fold in wild rice and bacon. Season to taste.

3. **Assemble the Eggs:**
   Pipe or spoon into whites.

4. **Garnish with Minnesota Flair:**
   Top with chopped bacon, a tiny drizzle of maple syrup, and fresh herbs.

Serving Vibe:

Serve on a rustic wood board with pine sprigs or autumn leaves nearby. Perfect for fall gatherings, cabin weekends, or a Minneapolis farmers market brunch.

Morgantown Pepper Jack & Smoked Sausage Deviled Eggs

Morgantown Pepper Jack & Smoked Sausage Deviled Eggs

Spicy, smoky, and full of mountain-town flavor. Deviled eggs filled with creamy yolk mixture blended with shredded pepper jack cheese and finely chopped smoked sausage. Each egg is topped with a thin slice or small crispy bite of smoked sausage and sprinkled with smoked paprika or chili powder

---

Why It's Uniquely Morgantown:

Morgantown's vibrant culinary scene blends Appalachian roots with modern flavors. This deviled egg features creamy yolks mixed with pepper jack cheese for a spicy kick and smoky local sausage for hearty depth. It's a perfect blend of comfort and flair for this bustling town.

Ingredients:

- 12 large eggs
- 1/3 cup mayonnaise
- 2 tbsp shredded pepper jack cheese
- 2 tbsp finely chopped smoked sausage (like kielbasa or local links)
- 1 tsp Dijon mustard
- Salt and pepper to taste

Topping:

- Thin slice of smoked sausage or small crispy sausage bite

- Sprinkle of smoked paprika or chili powder
- Optional: chopped fresh parsley or chives

Instructions:

1. **Boil and Cool the Eggs:**
   Standard boil, ice bath, peel.

2. **Make the Filling:**
   Mash yolks with mayo, cheese, sausage, and mustard. Season to taste.

3. **Assemble the Eggs:**
   Pipe or spoon into whites.

4. **Garnish with Mountain Flavor:**
   Top with sausage slice and sprinkle smoked paprika or chili powder.

Serving Vibe:

Serve on a rustic wooden board with local craft beers and mountain music playing. Perfect for tailgates, pub nights, or cozy gatherings.

Nashville Hot Chicken Deviled Eggs

Nashville Hot Chicken Deviled Eggs

These deviled eggs are bold and spicy—flavored with cayenne, a touch of hot sauce, and optionally crowned with a crispy chicken sliver for the full hot chicken vibe. Tennessee — the Volunteer State Inspired by Nashville hot chicken, this deviled egg is fiery and bold, with cayenne heat, pickle tang, and a crunch of seasoned breadcrumbs on top. It's a full-on Southern showstopper in one spicy bite.

Tennessee is famous for its music, mountains, and mouthwatering Southern food. From Memphis dry-rub barbecue to Nashville hot chicken, this state knows how to bring the heat and soul. For today's deviled egg, we're tipping our hat to **Nashville hot spice** with a fiery, Southern-fried twist that sings like a country guitar riff.

Ingredients:

- 12 large eggs
- 1/3 cup mayonnaise
- 1 tsp yellow mustard
- 1 tsp hot sauce (like Crystal or Tabasco)
- 1/4 tsp cayenne pepper (adjust to taste)
- Optional: pinch of brown sugar for sweet heat
- Optional: 6 small bites of crispy chicken or hot chicken skin
- Salt and pepper to taste

- Garnish: paprika, cayenne dusting, or hot chicken topper

Instructions:

1. **Boil and Cool Eggs:**
   Boil, rest, ice bath, peel.

2. **Make the Filling:**
   Mash yolks with mayo, mustard, hot sauce, cayenne, and sugar (if using). Season with salt and pepper. Taste and adjust heat.

3. **Assemble:**
   Pipe or spoon into egg whites.

4. **Garnish:**
   Sprinkle with cayenne or paprika—or top each egg with a **tiny Nashville hot chicken bite** for an irresistible Southern party hit.

Why It's Uniquely Tennessee:

Because no one does **heat with heart** like Tennessee. This deviled egg **cranks the flavor dial** with hot chicken inspiration, but balances it with that sweet Southern hospitality.

New Haven White Clam & Herb Deviled Eggs

New Haven White Clam & Herb Deviled Eggs

Elegant, oceanic, and surprisingly addictive. A deviled egg filled with a creamy, pale yolk mixture speckled with fresh herbs and topped with a tiny curl of clam meat, lemon zest, and a parsley leaf.

Why It's Uniquely Connecticut:

New Haven is famous for its white clam pizza—and this deviled egg channels that same briny, garlicky, herby magic. We use **finely chopped cooked clams**, **a hint of garlic**, **fresh parsley**, and **lemon zest** for brightness. It's coastal, classy, and a little unexpected—just like a Yale graduate who surfs on weekends.

Ingredients:
- 12 large eggs
- 1/3 cup mayonnaise
- 1 tsp lemon juice
- 1/2 tsp Dijon mustard
- 2 tbsp **finely chopped cooked clams** (canned or fresh, drained)
- 1/4 tsp garlic powder or a hint of minced garlic
- 1 tbsp chopped **fresh parsley**
- Salt and pepper to taste

Optional Enhancements: A pinch of crushed red pepper and or a bit of grated Parmesan

Garnish:

- Lemon zest
- Parsley leaf or microgreen
- Tiny clam meat curl, if desired

Instructions:

1. **Boil and Cool the Eggs:**
    - Standard: boil, rest, ice bath, peel.
2. **Make the Filling:**
    - Halve eggs, remove yolks.
    - Mash yolks with mayo, mustard, lemon juice, garlic, and clams.
    - Fold in parsley and season to taste.
3. **Assemble the Eggs:**
    - Pipe or spoon into whites.
4. **Garnish with a Taste of the Shore:**
    - Top with a lemon zest sprinkle and a parsley leaf or clam curl.

Serving Vibe:

Serve on a white platter with seashell accents, lemon wedges, and a crisp linen napkin—ideal for a beach house brunch or a seafood-forward picnic.

New Orleans Cajun Shrimp Remoulade Deviled Eggs

New Orleans Cajun Shrimp Remoulade Deviled Eggs

Spicy, creamy, and jazzy with Gulf Coast swagger. Deviled eggs filled with a creamy Cajun-spiced yolk mixture, each topped with a small shrimp coated in remoulade sauce. Garnishes include fresh parsley, paprika dusting, or a tiny lemon wedge

Why It's Uniquely New Orleans:

From beignets to étouffée, **New Orleans** cuisine is soulful, bold, and packed with layers of flavor. This deviled egg channels that same energy: a creamy yolk base spiced with Cajun seasoning and Creole mustard, topped with a juicy shrimp tossed in tangy remoulade sauce. It's Mardi Gras in a bite.

Ingredients:

- 12 large eggs
- 1/3 cup mayonnaise
- 1 tsp Creole mustard (or spicy brown mustard)
- 1/2 tsp lemon juice
- 1/2 tsp Cajun or Creole seasoning
- Salt and pepper to taste

Remoulade Shrimp Topper:

- 12 small cooked shrimp, peeled
- 2 tbsp mayonnaise

- 1 tsp ketchup or hot sauce
- 1/2 tsp lemon juice
- 1/2 tsp paprika
- Optional: dash of horseradish or minced garlic

Garnish: Fresh parsley, Paprika, Tiny slice of lemon or green onion

---

Instructions:

1. **Boil and Cool the Eggs:**
   Classic method: boil, rest, ice bath, peel.

2. **Make the Filling:**
   Mash yolks with mayo, mustard, lemon juice, and seasoning. Blend until smooth. Season to taste.

3. **Make the Shrimp Remoulade:**
   In a small bowl, toss shrimp with the remoulade sauce ingredients. Chill briefly.

4. **Assemble the Eggs:**
   Pipe or spoon filling into egg whites. Top each with one shrimp.

5. **Garnish with NOLA Flair:**
   Add a parsley leaf or sprinkle of paprika.

Serving Vibe:

Serve on a wrought-iron tray or Mardi Gras beads-lined platter with jazz playing in the background. Ideal for cocktail hour, brunch buffets, or any party that needs a little kick.

Newport Jazz & Clam Bake Deviled Eggs

Newport Jazz & Clam Bake Deviled Eggs

Smooth, soulful, and brimming with seaside spirit. Deviled eggs filled with creamy yolk mixed with finely chopped clams and a hint of Old Bay seasoning. Each egg is topped with crushed buttery oyster crackers and a small parsley leaf or microgreen.

Why It's Uniquely Providence:

Providence's jazz festival brings smooth rhythms to the city, and its coastal roots mean fresh seafood is always center stage. This deviled egg blends creamy yolks with tender clam meat and a hint of Old Bay, topped with a crunchy cracker crumble for that baked clam bake vibe—smooth, textured, and full of character.

Ingredients:

- 12 large eggs
- 1/3 cup mayonnaise
- 1 tsp Dijon mustard
- 1 tbsp finely chopped cooked clams
- 1/2 tsp Old Bay seasoning
- Salt and pepper to taste

Topping:

- Crushed oyster crackers or buttery cracker crumbs
- Small parsley leaf or microgreen

Instructions:

1. **Boil and Cool the Eggs:**
   Standard: boil, rest, ice bath, peel.

2. **Make the Filling:**
   Mash yolks with mayo, mustard, clams, and Old Bay. Season well.

3. **Assemble the Eggs:**
   Pipe or spoon filling into egg whites.

4. **Garnish with Jazz Flair:**
   Top with cracker crumbs and a fresh herb.

Serving Vibe:

Serve on a sleek black platter with candles and jazz records nearby. Perfect for an intimate concert or elegant coastal party.

Newark Jiburito-Inspired Deviled Eggs

Newark Jibarito-Inspired Deviled Eggs

Bold, tangy, and packed with Latin street food flavor. Deviled eggs filled with creamy yellow yolk mixed with garlic aioli and shredded grilled steak, speckled with fine white cheese. Each egg is topped with a thin pickle slice and chopped fresh cilantro.

Why It's Uniquely Newark:

Newark has a vibrant Latinx community and a growing food scene that honors Puerto Rican favorites like the **Jibarito**—a sandwich made with fried plantains instead of bread, layered with garlic mayo, steak, cheese, and pickles. This deviled egg adapts those flavors: creamy garlic aioli yolk, shredded steak or grilled skirt meat, a hint of cheese, and a tangy pickle topping.

Ingredients:

- 12 large eggs
- 1/4 cup mayonnaise
- 1 tbsp garlic aioli or roasted garlic mayo
- 1 tsp lime juice
- 1/2 cup shredded cooked skirt steak or flank steak (seasoned/grilled)
- 1 tbsp finely shredded cheese (like mozzarella or white cheddar)
- Salt and pepper to taste

Topping:

- Thin pickle slice or diced pickles
- Chopped fresh cilantro or parsley

Instructions:

1. **Boil and Cool the Eggs:**
   Standard: boil, ice bath, peel.

2. **Make the Filling:**
   Mash yolks with mayo, garlic aioli, and lime juice. Fold in shredded steak and cheese. Season to taste.

3. **Assemble the Eggs:**
   Pipe or spoon filling into whites.

4. **Garnish with Latin Flair:**
   Top with a pickle slice and chopped cilantro or parsley.

Serving Vibe:

Serve on a vibrant ceramic platter with street food energy—think colorful linens, small bowls of hot sauce, and upbeat music.

Niagara Falls Apple & Cheddar Deviled Eggs

Niagara Falls Apple & Cheddar Deviled Eggs

Sweet, sharp, and perfectly balanced with a nod to New York State's apple orchards. Deviled eggs filled with creamy yolk mixture blended with shredded sharp cheddar cheese, diced tart apple, and a touch of apple cider vinegar. Each egg is garnished with a thin apple slice fan and a sprinkle of shredded cheddar.

Why It's Uniquely Niagara Falls:

New York State is famous for its apple orchards, and Niagara Falls blends those fresh orchard flavors with sharp cheddar cheese, creating a deviled egg that's both crisp and comforting.

Ingredients:

- 12 large eggs
- 1/4 cup mayonnaise
- 1 tbsp apple cider vinegar
- 1/4 cup shredded sharp cheddar cheese
- 1/4 cup finely diced tart apple (such as Granny Smith)
- Salt and pepper to taste

Garnish:

- Thin apple slice or small apple fan
- Shredded cheddar
- Optional: sprinkle of cinnamon or fresh thyme

Instructions:

1. **Boil and Cool the Eggs:**
   Standard boil, ice bath, peel.

2. **Make the Filling:**
   Mash yolks with mayo, vinegar, cheddar, and diced apple. Season to taste.

3. **Assemble the Eggs:**
   Pipe or spoon filling into whites.

4. **Garnish with Orchard Freshness:**
   Top with a thin apple slice, shredded cheddar, and optional cinnamon or thyme.

Serving Vibe:

Serve on a rustic wooden board with views or imagery of Niagara Falls and fresh apple cider. Perfect for autumn gatherings or scenic picnics.

Omaha Steakhouse Deviled Eggs

Omaha Steakhouse Deviled Eggs

Rich, hearty, and full of Midwest boldness. Deviled eggs filled with creamy yolk mixed with horseradish and Dijon mustard, speckled with finely chopped smoked steak or roast beef. Each egg is topped with additional beef pieces and a sprinkle of coarse cracked black pepper and fresh parsley or chives.

Why It's Uniquely Omaha:

Omaha is famous for its beef, and these deviled eggs channel that steakhouse vibe with a creamy yolk base infused with horseradish and topped with finely chopped smoked steak or roast beef. A touch of cracked black pepper adds a savory kick—perfect for a city proud of its meat-centric traditions.

Ingredients:

- 12 large eggs
- 1/3 cup mayonnaise
- 1 tsp prepared horseradish
- 1 tsp Dijon mustard
- 2–3 tbsp finely chopped smoked steak or roast beef
- Salt and black pepper to taste

Topping:

- Extra chopped beef

- Coarse cracked black pepper
- Optional: fresh parsley or chive

Instructions:

1. **Boil and Cool the Eggs:**
   Standard boil, ice bath, peel.

2. **Make the Filling:**
   Mash yolks with mayo, horseradish, and mustard. Fold in chopped beef. Season with salt and pepper.

3. **Assemble the Eggs:**
   Pipe or spoon into whites.

4. **Garnish Omaha Style:**
   Top with more beef, cracked pepper, and herbs.

Serving Vibe:

Serve on a dark wooden board or steakhouse platter with steak knives, cocktail sauce, and a glass of full-bodied red wine or craft beer.

Philly Cheesesteak Deviled Eggs

Philly Cheesesteak Deviled Eggs

Welcome to Pennsylvania, where food comes in two speeds: Philly fast (*cheesesteak, pretzel, hoagie, repeat*) and Amish slow (*pickled, buttered, smoked, and blessed.*) So how do we build a deviled egg that's both hearty and hometown-proud?

We take a creamy yolk base, add sharp mustard, a touch of cream cheese (hello, cheesesteak), and top it with a crisped sliver of roast beef or pretzel crumble. Whether you're dining under a Lancaster barn beam or a Liberty Bell, this egg fits.

Why It's Uniquely Pennsylvania:

Pennsylvania is the **birthplace of American pretzels**, and mustard is never far behind. This deviled egg captures the salty, tangy joy of **a Philly pretzel cart snack** or **Lancaster County church supper**, all in one bite.

Ingredients:

- 12 large eggs
- 1/3 cup mayonnaise

- 1 tbsp coarse-grain mustard (stone-ground or spicy brown)
- 1 tsp apple cider vinegar or pickle brine
- Salt and black pepper to taste
- Optional: pinch of sugar or celery seed
- Garnish: **crushed pretzels**, chives, or a tiny dollop of mustard

Instructions:

1. **Boil and Cool the Eggs:**
   Boil, rest, ice bath, peel.

2. **Make the Filling:**
   Mash yolks with mayo, coarse mustard, and vinegar. Adjust seasoning to taste—add a touch of sugar or celery seed for that Pennsylvania Dutch vibe.

3. **Assemble:**
   Pipe or spoon into whites.

4. **Garnish:**
   Top with a few crushed hard pretzel bits and a flick of chive. Optional: add a tiny mustard dollop for drama.

Portland Lobster & Brown Butter Deviled Eggs

Portland Lobster & Brown Butter Deviled Eggs

Rich, nutty, and refined—like lobster in a little black dress. Deviled eggs filled with a creamy yolk mixture infused with brown butter and chopped lobster meat. Each egg is topped with a drizzle of brown butter, a small sprig of microgreens or tarragon, and a delicate garnish like a paprika dusting or edible flower petal.

Why It's Uniquely Portland, Maine:

This version leans into **brown butter elegance**—an upscale touch that Maine's foodie scene would love. It highlights the sweetness of lobster, the richness of browned butter, and a squeeze of lemon to brighten it all. Think harbor chic meets downtown fine dining.

Ingredients:

- 12 large eggs
- 1/4 cup mayonnaise
- 1 tsp Dijon mustard
- 1 tsp lemon juice
- 2 tbsp unsalted butter (browned)
- 2 oz lobster meat, chopped (claw or tail)
- Salt and white pepper to taste

Optional Garnish:

- Tiny drizzle of brown butter
- Microgreens or tarragon
- Paprika or edible flower petal

Instructions:

1. **Boil and Cool the Eggs:**
   Standard method: boil, rest, ice bath, peel.

2. **Brown the Butter:**
   In a small pan, melt butter and cook until golden brown and nutty-smelling. Let cool slightly.

3. **Make the Filling:**
   Mash yolks with mayo, mustard, lemon juice, and a spoonful of brown butter. Fold in lobster. Season to taste with salt and white pepper.

4. **Assemble:**
   Pipe or spoon mixture into egg whites.

5. **Garnish with Finesse:**
   Drizzle with a touch of brown butter and top with microgreens or a small tarragon leaf.

Serving Vibe:

Serve on white stoneware with coastal textures—smooth shells, sea glass, or a linen napkin in the frame. Elegant enough for a seaside wedding, dinner party, or foodie tasting menu.

Portsmouth Clam & Chive Deviled Egs

Portsmouth Clam & Chive Deviled Eggs

Fresh, briny, and simple—New England coastal goodness. Deviled eggs filled with a creamy yolk mixture blended with chopped clams, crispy bacon, and fresh thyme. Each egg is topped with a bacon crumble, crushed oyster cracker, or micro-thyme sprig.

Why It's Uniquely Portsmouth:

Portsmouth's location on the Atlantic means fresh clams and seafood are always front and center. This deviled egg is light and bright with chopped clams, fresh chives, and a touch of lemon to bring the coast to your plate.

Ingredients:

- 12 large eggs
- 1/3 cup mayonnaise
- 1 tsp lemon juice
- 1/2 tsp Dijon mustard
- 2 tbsp finely chopped cooked clams (canned or fresh)
- 1 tbsp chopped fresh chives
- Salt and pepper to taste

Garnish:

- Chopped chives
- Lemon zest
- Small clam or parsley leaf

Instructions:

1. **Boil and Cool the Eggs:**
   Standard: boil, rest, ice bath, peel.

2. **Make the Filling:**
   Mash yolks with mayo, mustard, and lemon juice. Fold in chopped clams and chives. Season to taste.

3. **Assemble the Eggs:**
   Pipe or spoon into whites.

4. **Garnish with Coastal Freshness:**
   Top with chopped chives, lemon zest, or a parsley leaf.

Serving Vibe:

Serve on a white ceramic plate or driftwood board with nautical accents and fresh sea air vibes.

Rehoboth Beach Crab & Old Bay Deviled Eggs

Rehoboth Beach Crab & Old Bay Deviled Eggs

Fresh, zesty, and seaside-inspired. **Deviled eggs filled with creamy yolk mixture blended with tender blue crab meat and Old Bay seasoning. Each egg is topped with a sprinkle of Old Bay and fresh chives or parsley.**

Why It's Uniquely Rehoboth Beach:

Rehoboth Beach is famous for its succulent blue crab and the signature Old Bay seasoning that brings the flavors of the Chesapeake Bay to life. This deviled egg blends creamy yolks with tender crab meat and a dash of Old Bay, topped with a sprinkle of the iconic seasoning and a fresh herb.

Ingredients:

- 12 large eggs
- 1/3 cup mayonnaise
- 1 tsp Dijon mustard
- 3 oz lump blue crab meat, picked over for shells
- 1/2 tsp Old Bay seasoning (plus more for garnish)
- Salt and pepper to taste

Garnish:

- Sprinkle of Old Bay
- Fresh chives or parsley

Instructions:

1. **Boil and Cool the Eggs:**
   Standard: boil, rest, ice bath, peel.

2. **Make the Filling:**
   Mash yolks with mayo, mustard, and Old Bay. Gently fold in crab meat. Season to taste.

3. **:Assemble the Eggs:**
   Pipe or spoon filling into whites.

4. **Garnish with Coastal Flair:**
   Sprinkle extra Old Bay and fresh herbs on top.

Serving Vibe:

Serve on a light blue or white platter with nautical décor and a seaside breeze. Perfect for beach parties or summer gatherings.

Richmond Ham & Pimento Deviled Eggs

Richmond Ham & Pimento Deviled Eggs

Savory, creamy, and bursting with Southern flavor. Deviled eggs filled with creamy yolk mixture blended with finely chopped Virginia ham and pimento cheese. Each egg is garnished with a small slice of pimento and chopped chives or parsley, with a light sprinkle of smoked paprika.

Why It's Uniquely Richmond:

Richmond is famous for its cured ham and love of classic Southern ingredients. This deviled egg features creamy yolks blended with finely chopped Virginia ham and tangy pimento cheese, delivering a rich, comforting bite that pays homage to the region's culinary roots.

Ingredients:

- 12 large eggs
- 1/3 cup mayonnaise
- 2 tbsp finely chopped Virginia ham (cured or smoked)
- 1/4 cup pimento cheese
- 1 tsp Dijon mustard
- Salt and pepper to taste

Garnish:

- Small pimento slice

- Chopped chives or parsley
- Optional: sprinkle of smoked paprika

Instructions:

1. **Boil and Cool the Eggs:**
   Standard method: boil, rest, ice bath, peel.

2. **Make the Filling:**
   Mash yolks with mayo, mustard, ham, and pimento cheese. Season well.

3. **Assemble the Eggs:**
   Pipe or spoon filling into whites.

4. **Garnish with Southern Flair:**
   Top with a pimento slice, fresh herbs, and optional smoked paprika.

Serving Vibe:

Serve on a vintage ceramic platter with Southern sweet tea or a light cocktail. Perfect for garden parties or historic home gatherings.

Salt Lake City Honey & Sage Deviled Eggs

Salt Lake City Honey & Sage Deviled Eggs

Sweet, herbal, and delightfully unexpected. Deviled eggs filled with creamy yolk mixture blended with local honey and finely chopped fresh sage. Each egg is topped with a small sage leaf and a delicate drizzle of honey.

Why It's Uniquely Salt Lake City:

Utah is the Beehive State, known for its honey and natural beauty. This deviled egg pairs creamy yolks with a drizzle of local honey and fresh sage for a bright, sweet-herbal contrast. It's simple, elegant, and deeply rooted in Utah's landscape.

Ingredients:

- 12 large eggs
- 1/3 cup mayonnaise
- 1 tsp Dijon mustard
- 1 tbsp local honey
- 1 tsp finely chopped fresh sage
- Salt and pepper to taste

Garnish:

- Small sage leaf

- Drizzle of honey
- Optional: sprinkle of toasted nuts or seeds

Instructions:

1. **Boil and Cool the Eggs:**
   Standard: boil, rest, ice bath, peel.

2. **Make the Filling:**
   Mash yolks with mayo, mustard, honey, and sage. Season to taste.

3. **Assemble the Eggs:**
   Pipe or spoon filling into whites.

4. **Garnish with Beehive Charm:**
   Top with a sage leaf, honey drizzle, and optional nuts or seeds.

Serving Vibe:

Serve on a clean white plate with rustic wooden accents and fresh herbs nearby. Perfect for mountain brunches or garden parties.

San Francisco Sourdough & Dungeness Crab Deviled Eggs

San Francisco Sourdough & Dungeness Crab Deviled Eggs

Fresh, tangy, and brimming with Bay Area charm. Deviled eggs filled with creamy yolk mixture blended with fresh Dungeness crab meat and tangy sourdough mustard. Each egg is topped with toasted sourdough bread crumbs and garnished with fresh dill or chives.

Why It's Uniquely San Francisco:

San Francisco is famous for its tangy sourdough bread and sweet, tender Dungeness crab. This deviled egg blends creamy yolks with crab meat and a touch of tangy sourdough mustard, topped with toasted sourdough crumbs for crunch—capturing the essence of the Bay Area in a bite.

Ingredients:

- 12 large eggs
- 1/3 cup mayonnaise
- 3 oz fresh Dungeness crab meat, picked over shells
- 1 tsp sourdough mustard or Dijon mustard
- 1/4 cup toasted sourdough bread crumbs
- Salt and pepper to taste

Garnish:

- Toasted sourdough crumbs
- Fresh dill or chives

Instructions:

1. **Boil and Cool the Eggs:**
   Standard boil, rest, ice bath, peel.

2. **Make the Filling:**
   Mash yolks with mayo, sourdough mustard, and crab meat. Season to taste.

3. **Assemble the Eggs:**
   Pipe or spoon filling into whites.

4. **Garnish with Bay Area Flair:**
   Top with toasted sourdough crumbs and fresh herbs.

Serving Vibe:

Serve on a modern ceramic platter with views or imagery of the Golden Gate Bridge and a crisp white wine or local craft beer. Perfect for elegant coastal gatherings.

Santa Fe Tomatillo & Cilantro Deviled Eggs

Santa Fe Tomatillo & Cilantro Deviled Eggs

Bright, zesty, and refreshingly green—like a summer in the high desert. Deviled eggs filled with a bright green, creamy yolk mixture flecked with finely chopped roasted tomatillos and fresh cilantro. Each egg is garnished with a small wedge or thin slice of tomatillo, a cilantro leaf, and a light dusting of smoked paprika or chili powder.

Why It's Uniquely Santa Fe:

Tomatillos bring a tangy brightness to many New Mexican dishes—from salsa verde to enchiladas verdes. Paired with fresh cilantro and a hint of lime, this deviled egg offers a cool, herby, and slightly tart twist that captures the spirit of Santa Fe's vibrant food culture.

Ingredients:

- 12 large eggs
- 1/3 cup mayonnaise
- 1/4 cup finely chopped **roasted or fresh tomatillos**
- 1 tbsp chopped fresh cilantro
- 1 tsp lime juice
- 1/2 tsp ground cumin
- Salt and pepper to taste

Garnish:

- Small tomatillo wedge or thin slice
- Cilantro leaf
- Optional: pinch of smoked paprika or chili powder

Instructions:

1. **Boil and Cool the Eggs:**
   Boil, ice bath, peel.

2. **Make the Filling:**
   Mash yolks with mayo, tomatillos, cilantro, lime juice, and cumin. Season to taste.

3. **Assemble the Eggs:**
   Pipe or spoon filling into egg whites.

4. **Garnish with a Southwest Kick:**
   Top with a tomatillo wedge, cilantro leaf, and optional sprinkle of smoked paprika or chili powder.

Serving Vibe:

Serve on a vibrant, colorful ceramic plate with woven textiles and rustic desert décor. Perfect for sunny brunches or lively Southwestern gatherings.

St. Louis Toasted Ravioli & Provel Deviled Eggs

St. Louis Toasted Ravioli & Provel Deviled Eggs

Crunchy, cheesy, and totally indulgent. Deviled eggs filled with creamy yolk mixed with shredded Provel cheese and herbs, piped into whites. Each egg is topped with a mini crispy toasted ravioli or a sprinkle of golden toasted breadcrumbs.

Why It's Uniquely St. Louis:

Toasted ravioli is a St. Louis invention—crispy, golden, and served with zesty marinara. This deviled egg takes that concept, stuffing the yolks with Provel cheese (a creamy, smoky St. Louis staple), garlic, and herbs, then topping each egg with a mini crispy ravioli chip or a breadcrumb crunch. It's indulgence meets city classic.

Ingredients:

- 12 large eggs
- 1/3 cup mayonnaise
- 2 tbsp cream cheese
- 1/4 cup shredded **Provel cheese** (or a mix of cheddar, Swiss, and provolone)
- 1 tsp garlic powder
- 1 tbsp finely chopped fresh parsley
- Salt and pepper to taste

Topping:

- Mini crispy toasted ravioli or toasted breadcrumbs
- Optional: drizzle of marinara or sprinkle of Parmesan

Instructions:

1. **Boil and Cool the Eggs:**
   Standard boil, rest, ice bath, peel.

2. **Make the Filling:**
   Mash yolks with mayo, cream cheese, shredded Provel, garlic powder, and parsley. Season to taste.

3. **Assemble the Eggs:**
   Pipe or spoon the creamy filling into whites.

4. **Top with St. Louis Crunch:**
   Garnish with a crispy toasted ravioli chip or a sprinkle of toasted breadcrumbs. Optional marinara drizzle.

Serving Vibe:

Serve on a metal tray or red gingham napkins, perfect for a local tavern or game night spread.

Sioux Falls Bison Chili Deviled Eggs

Sioux Falls Bison Chili Deviled Eggs

Savory, spicy, and deeply satisfying—a taste of the plains in every bite. Deviled eggs filled with creamy yolk mixed with smoky bison chili and chili powder. Each egg is topped with shredded sharp cheddar, a sprinkle of chili powder or smoked paprika, and optional sliced jalapeño or chopped green onion.

Why It's Uniquely Sioux Falls:

Bison chili combines lean, flavorful bison meat with classic chili spices—perfect for a region where game and hearty stews rule. This deviled egg infuses creamy yolks with smoky, spiced bison chili, topped with shredded cheddar and a dash of chili powder for a fiery finish.

Ingredients:

- 12 large eggs
- 1/3 cup mayonnaise
- 1/3 cup cooked bison chili (no beans or drained well)
- 1 tsp chili powder
- Salt and pepper to taste

Topping:

- Shredded sharp cheddar
- Dash of chili powder or smoked paprika
- Optional: sliced jalapeño or chopped green onion

Instructions:

1. **Boil and Cool the Eggs:**
   Standard boil, ice bath, peel.

2. **Make the Filling:**
   Mash yolks with mayo, chili, and chili powder. Season to taste.

3. **Assemble the Eggs:**
   Pipe or spoon filling into whites.

4. **Garnish with Heat:**
   Top with shredded cheddar, chili powder, and optional jalapeño or green onion.

Serving Vibe:

Serve on a rustic wooden platter with craft beer or bold red wine. Perfect for game day or hearty Midwestern gatherings.

Tucson Roasted Poblano & Queso Fresco Deviled Eggs

Tucson Roasted Poblano & Queso Fresco Deviled Eggs

Creamy, smoky, and sun-baked Southwest style. A deviled egg filled with creamy yolk mixed with green flecks of roasted poblano and cilantro, topped with crumbled queso fresco and a tiny curl of pickled red onion.

Why It's Uniquely Tucson:

Tucson's food is shaped by the Sonoran Desert—think roasted peppers, creamy cheeses, and spices balanced with citrus or herbs. This deviled egg brings the heat with **roasted poblano peppers**, cools it with **queso fresco**, and adds **lime and cilantro** for a refreshing, modern twist. Rustic meets refined.

Ingredients:

- 12 large eggs
- 1/3 cup mayonnaise
- 1/2 tsp Dijon mustard
- 1 tsp lime juice
- 1–2 tbsp **finely diced roasted poblano pepper** (peeled and deseeded)
- 1 tbsp chopped fresh cilantro
- Salt and pepper to taste

Toppings: Crumbled **queso fresco and k**ime zest or a cilantro leaf

Optional:

- Pinch of cumin or smoked paprika
- Thin sliver of pickled red onion for extra color

Instructions:

1. **Boil and Cool the Eggs:**
   - Standard boil, ice bath, peel.
2. **Make the Filling:**
   - Slice eggs and remove yolks.
   - Mash yolks with mayo, mustard, and lime juice.
   - Fold in roasted poblano and cilantro. Season to taste.
3. **Assemble the Eggs:**
   - Pipe or spoon into egg whites.
4. **Top with Desert Flair:**
   - Garnish with crumbled queso fresco, lime zest, and a cilantro leaf or sliver of pickled onion.

Serving Vibe:

Perfect with tamales, margaritas, or grilled street corn at a backyard brunch or desert rooftop party.

Tulsa Chicken-Fried Steak & White Gravy Deviled Eggs

Tulsa Chicken-Fried Steak & White Gravy Deviled Eggs

Comforting, indulgent, and unapologetically Southern. Deviled eggs filled with creamy yolk mixture blended with white gravy flavors and finely chopped chicken-fried steak. Each egg is topped with crispy beef bits and a small drizzle of white gravy or ranch dressing.

Why It's Uniquely Tulsa:

Chicken-fried steak with creamy white gravy is a beloved Oklahoma comfort dish. This deviled egg brings that indulgence to bite-size form—rich yolks blended with white gravy flavors, topped with crispy beef bits and a drizzle of gravy-inspired sauce.

Ingredients:

- 12 large eggs
- 1/3 cup mayonnaise
- 1 tbsp white gravy or cream gravy (prepared or homemade)
- 1 tsp Dijon mustard
- 2 tbsp finely chopped cooked chicken-fried steak or beef
- Salt and pepper to taste

Topping:

- Crispy beef bits or crushed pork rinds
- Small drizzle of white gravy or ranch dressing
- Optional chopped parsley

Instructions:

1. **Boil and Cool the Eggs:**
   Standard boil, rest, ice bath, peel.

2. **Make the Filling:**
   Mash yolks with mayo, gravy, and mustard. Fold in chopped steak. Season to taste.

3. **Assemble the Eggs:**
   Pipe or spoon filling into whites.

4. **Garnish with Tulsa Flair:**
   Top with crispy beef bits and a drizzle of gravy or ranch.

Serving Vibe:

Serve on a rustic wooden platter with Mason jars of sweet tea or local craft beer. Perfect for Southern dinners or cozy gatherings.

Virginia Beach Old Bay & Fried Clam Deviled Eggs

Virginia Beach Old Bay & Fried Clam Deviled Eggs

Crispy, zesty, and packed with seaside flavor.

Why It's Uniquely Virginia Beach:

Virginia Beach cuisine celebrates fresh seafood with a nod to Old Bay seasoning and fried clams. This deviled egg features creamy yolks blended with a touch of Old Bay, topped with crunchy fried clam bits and a sprinkle of paprika for a perfect beach bite.

Ingredients:

- 12 large eggs
- 1/3 cup mayonnaise
- 1 tsp Dijon mustard
- 1/2 tsp Old Bay seasoning (plus more for garnish)
- 2 tbsp finely chopped fried clams or clam strips
- Salt and pepper to taste

Topping:

- Crunchy fried clam bits

- Sprinkle of paprika
- Fresh parsley or chives

Instructions:

1. **Boil and Cool the Eggs:**
   Standard boil, ice bath, peel.

2. **Make the Filling:**
   Mash yolks with mayo, mustard, and Old Bay. Fold in fried clam bits. Season to taste.

3. **Assemble the Eggs:**
   Pipe or spoon filling into whites.

4. **Garnish with Beach Flair:**
   Top with fried clam bits, paprika, and fresh herbs.

Serving Vibe:

Serve on a casual wooden board with beachy décor and cold beers or citrus cocktails. Perfect for boardwalk parties or summer beach days.

Coffee & Vanilla-Infused Egg Whites + Maple Bacon Filling deviled egg gets the Chef's kiss.

Coffee & Vanilla-Infused Egg Whites + Maple Bacon Filling

This is a fancy egg where the egg white is infused with flavor and perfectly enhances the flavor of the deviled egg.

Ingredients

Egg White Infusion:

- 6 large eggs, hard-boiled and peeled
- 1 cup strong brewed coffee, cooled
- 1/2 tsp vanilla extract

Filling:

- 6 egg yolks
- 2 tbsp mayonnaise
- 1 tbsp finely crumbled bacon (vegetarian bacon optional)
- 1 tsp pure maple syrup
- Salt and pepper to taste

Garnish:

- Bacon bits or small maple drizzle

Instructions

1. Mix cooled coffee and vanilla. Soak egg whites 1–2 hours in fridge.
2. Mash yolks with mayo, bacon, maple syrup, salt, and pepper until creamy.
3. Remove whites, pat dry, fill with yolk mixture.
4. Garnish with bacon bits or a light maple drizzle.

*Bonus: Maple Martini Recipe to pair with the luxurious Coffee infused deviled egg.

Maple Espresso Martini

Ingredients (makes 1 cocktail):

- 2 oz vodka (vanilla vodka optional for extra depth)
- 1 oz freshly brewed espresso (or cold brew concentrate)
- 1/2 oz Kahlúa (or another coffee liqueur)
- 1/2 oz pure maple syrup (adjust to taste)
- Ice
- Coffee beans, for garnish (optional)
- Small amount of maple syrup for drizzling (optional)

Instructions:

1. Brew your espresso and let it cool slightly (or use cold brew concentrate for ease).
2. In a cocktail shaker, add:
    - Vodka
    - Kahlúa
    - Espresso

- Maple syrup
- A generous handful of ice

3. Shake **vigorously** for 15–20 seconds to create a smooth crema.

4. Strain into a chilled martini glass.

5. Garnish with **three coffee beans** (for health, wealth, and happiness 😊).

6. (Optional) Use a cocktail stick or fine spoon to drizzle a swirl of maple syrup on top for that dramatic look.

Optional Twists:

- Add a splash of **bourbon** instead of vodka for a smokier, more robust version.
- Rim the glass with **maple sugar** or **espresso powder** for extra flair.

Mocktail Maple Espresso Martini

Mocktail Maple Espresso Martini

Not everyone drinks alcohol, so here you go, a delicious mocktail version of that gorgeous drink. It's bold, rich, and sophisticated — perfect to sip beside your coffee-vanilla eggs.

Ingredients (makes 1 mocktail):

- 2 oz cold brew concentrate or strong chilled espresso
- 1 oz brewed chicory tea (or a splash of non-alcoholic coffee liqueur alternative, optional)
- 1/2 oz pure maple syrup
- 1/4 tsp vanilla extract (for depth and warmth)
- Ice
- Coffee beans, for garnish
- Optional: non-dairy foam or whipped aquafaba for topping (for that frothy crema look)

Instructions:

1. Brew and chill your espresso and (if using) chicory tea.

2. In a cocktail shaker, combine:
    - Cold brew or espresso
    - Chicory tea or alcohol-free liqueur
    - Maple syrup
    - Vanilla extract
    - A handful of ice
3. Shake vigorously until frothy and well chilled.
4. Strain into a chilled martini glass.
5. Garnish with **3 coffee beans** or a delicate swirl of maple syrup.

Optional Fancy Toppings:

- Frothy **aquafaba foam** (chickpea brine shaken vigorously with maple syrup and a touch of cream of tartar)
- Sprinkle of **cocoa powder** or **espresso dust**

Thank you for purchasing and enjoying this recipe book. There is a sequel to this book entitled, **Veggie Eggies:** *Vegetarian Deviled Egg Recipes*. In that book you will find vegetarian recipes as well as more infused egg recipes and mocktails to make your entertaining more exciting. The first book of this series is called, **State of the Egg:** *50 Deviled Egg Recipes from 50 States*.

Also, look for **The Global Egg** where you'll find deviled egg recipes featuring global spices, and flavors for all tastes & occasions.

It's been a pleasure. See you in the next book.

Marlene Miles

Avid Home Cook

www.ingramcontent.com/pod-product-compliance
Lightning Source LLC
Chambersburg PA
CBHW080245170426
43192CB00014BA/2576